The Soul of a Tree

David A. Schneck

BookLocker
Trenton, Georgia

Hardcover ISBN: 978-1-64719-595-3
Paperback ISBN: 978-1-64719-596-0
Ebook ISBN: 978-1-64719-597-7

Published by BookLocker.com, Inc., Trenton, Georgia.

This book is a work of historical fiction. Many names, characters, places, and incidents are the product of the author's imagination, but used within the historical framework of the United States.

Cover art courtesy of Herbert K. Ryder/Basking Ridge Presbyterian Church.

Chapter art design by Kate McGowan Schultz. Additional art work by Paige Anderson.

Printed on acid-free paper.

BookLocker.com, Inc.
2021

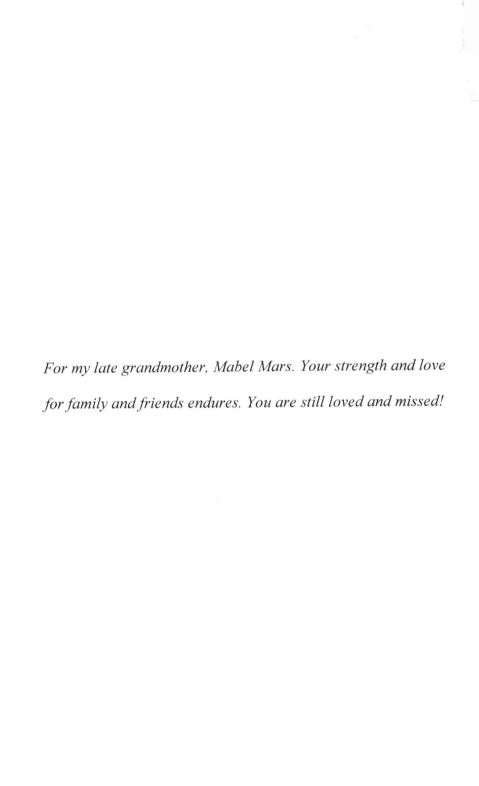

For my late grandmother, Mabel Mars. Your strength and love

for family and friends endures. You are still loved and missed!

CHAPTER ONE

May all I say and all I think be in harmony with thee, God within me, God beyond me, maker of the trees.
-- *Native American Prayer of Harmony*

So, a wedding. A good surprise. But then, not a surprise. Their announcement was almost predictable. The couple hugged and kissed. The wedding was going to be in the fall. A beautiful time of year. The trees would be in full blaze.

Dan Gobin liked Peggy Weida and approved of the match. It was clear to anyone who had eyes, that Dan's son, Adam was happy. Happiest he'd been in years. Adam & Peggy spent so much time together and had fallen in love right in front of Dan's eyes. And Adam and Peggy had eyes only for each other. They had known each other for only a year, but they were a great pair. *Just like me and...*but no, Dan wasn't going to go there.

Adam had been quiet and restless ever since his mother died. Recently, there was a light in his eyes and a steady tone in his voice. He laughed more, teased Dan more. At work, Adam was focused and determined. He was a man with a plan.

Peggy was good for Adam. Pulled him out of his cocoon of grief and into the world of the living. She needed him too. A super organized teacher, she had Adam to teach her to let her hair down and smell the roses. After she arranged them in alphabetical order by species.

Dan hugged Peggy and then Adam. "Go tell grandma." The two ran out the door and climbed into Adam's truck. They headed down the street to inform Dan's mother. Although she probably knew already, the courtesy of showing her the ring and talking about dates and venues needed to be done.

Dan watched the couple drive down the road. His gaze fell on the trees. It felt natural to compare everything (life, death, weddings, and funerals) to the life of the trees in the front yard. He planted the row of three when Adam was a baby, they were now sturdy, 15-foot leafy green oaks, full of life. Barring disease and invasive Gypsy Moth, they'd be around long after Adam buried him. Trees seem to outlive everyone in his family.

The phone rang. Dan answered the phone and smiled. It was his friend Ken on the other end of the line. "Well, hey good to hear from you. What trees are you climbing these days?" Dan settled into a large chair by the window. "Wait a minute, what tree are you taking down? That thing's massive!" He exclaimed. "Me? You want me to help?" Dan rubbed his head. "I don't know. Let me think about it. That oak has got to be 500 years old." He paused and listened to the voice on the other end that corrected him. "Wow, it's over 600? This is not going to be easy."

1487

The Ridge Oak Tree survived many seasons, endured hungry rabbits gnaws, buck antler rubs, ice storms, drought, hurricanes and the hands of man. The Navesink chief rubbed the sturdy tree's bark. The tree loomed over him; long limbs stretched nearly as wide as it was tall. And it still had many seasons to grow. There was so much life in this oak.

He embraced the trunk, flattening his body along its rough surface. He placed his ear against its grayish brown wrinkled skin and listened. He listened for its song.

It was not unusual for large trees to be spied in the forest which were taller than many men. Yet, this tree had a special place a bit apart from the pine grove and close to the middle of a meadow. Chief Ockanickon had marked that two suns rose and set on his journey from the Hunting Grounds to the Great Swamp.

Yes, he had heard the song about the massive tree from his grandmother who had heard those songs from her grandmother. As long as the Navesink had circled the Great Swamp, the tree was honored. It was one thing to hear about the tree, but it is another thing to be near the tree to see its size and to be touching such a great living thing. The bark felt warm under his hands. Days of summer sun heated the tree's tough outer skin.

Everything nature had thrown at the tree to destroy it only succeeded at making it stronger and hardier. As though the tree had learned its lesson and weathered catastrophes well. The chief looked up. The tree was not very tall but was wide. It avoided any negative encounter with strong, high winds by establishing a very wide and sturdy base.

He touched the bark and waited for the tree to speak its name to him. A breeze brushed by and teased the branches. It was then, the tree whispered its name. And sang its song to the man.

I was here before you.
I will be here with you.
I will live here after you.

Then Chief Ockanickon reached up and pinched off a leaf from one of the tree's low branches. He gathered acorns into his deer hide bag. He touched the bark again and blessed the tree. He sang the tree song once more with its name. He made sure to salute those who would touch the tree. He saluted those who would come from the south, the north, the east and the west.

Then raising his voice in prayer, he asked for protection for the tree so that it would see his grandchildren and their grandchildren. And he promised himself, he would tell his people, if they came to touch the tree, and if they were of a good heart, they would be touched. Those who blessed the tree would bless themselves. Those who would do harm to the tree would do harm to themselves. This too, he vowed would be passed along to all in the Ockanickon's tribe. The great tree's song was to be respected. Because the tree - would give a small part of its soul to live on within the person who touched it.

Chief Ockanickon was anxious to be on his way. Rumors of the Tidewater People coming north were getting louder. It wasn't right that all the Lenape who were once one people, are now factions, fighting amongst themselves while the *Nanticokes* from many different lands were slowly but surely clinging to the coast and then moving westward into Ramapough lands.

He had heard from a great matriarch that she had watched the *hakihet* clear an entire forest within a season. From the sea to the first hill, said the old woman, it was all gone. Much was burned; the rest used for fencing and rafts.

Once more Chief Ockanickon embraced the tree. He sang his song into its bark. He gave the tree his blessing and obtained one in return. He sang the song of his tribe into its veins. He wanted to make sure that no hand would destroy the great tree before it was ready to pass away.

Stepping away he looked up and saw a flock of wintering geese fly above the great tree's branches. Time to go.

He couldn't resist gathering more acorns and tucking them into his pouch for planting. He also clipped a few more green sticks of the tree from the lower limbs to keep for grafting.

Though this tree was slow growing, he would plant them. He would also plant as many of the acorns as he could and give some as gifts. He would never see them mature into their magnificent adulthood. The Great Oak Tree and its saplings will outlive him. Its song can only be enjoyed while a man is alive.

Chief Ockanickon - travelled west and north from the tree and though no one impeded his travel, he felt he was being followed. A presence walked alongside of him. The spirit of the tree was with him in his hand that touched the sap and in the acorns that were in his pouch.

For one hundred years, Chief Ockanickon and the great white oak tree were sung about in the long houses of the Navesink, Kechemeche and Delaware tribes. And although many saplings grew to be substantial, they were prevented from becoming as large as the great oak. It was as though the Great Oak Tree overshadowed its rivals.

This proved to the descendants of Chief Ockanickon that he had found the sacred tree, the tree of trees. Many tribes made a pilgrimage to the Great Oak Tree to touch its bark, sing its great song and gather acorns which it shed generously.

CHAPTER TWO

Whisper your sins to a tree, and you'll always be forgiven.
--Lady Marie Louise Brigette LeMen, last statement pre-guillotine, 1793

She stomped down the stairs, muttering under her breath. "Good lord, how many times do I have to hear 'no' from that boy?" Lillian Gobin bit back a few other choice words. *And why on earth do I need a man to tell me what I should or shouldn't wear to my own grandson's wedding? I've already picked out three dresses!*

"And, this one?" She was sure her son would approve of the light green chiffon.

Dan Gobin said nothing, just shook his head, *no.*

Back upstairs she went. She struggled into her last dress. She didn't even bother to zip it all the way up. In stocking feet, she went down the stairs ready to defend her choice.

"Now listen—,"

Dan interrupted. "Oh yeah, I like that one." He nodded. "I think it looks great on you."

"You do?"

"Yeah, Adam will love it too."

"Oh, well I--,"

"We gotta go Mom." Dan guided her back upstairs. "I'll get the car around front. You just get," he paused. "Shoes or something."

Oh no! Shoes! And I need a purse! She didn't stomp this time. She ran up the stairs. Rummaging through her closet, nothing worked, matched or complimented the deep salmon silk dress. Nothing. In desperation, she yanked the pull string for the attic trap and shimmied up the stepladder. *In my good dress, no less!* Kneeling on the floor, she opened a battered clothes trunk. Her mother, God rest her soul, had a collection of accessories that just might work. Flipping through the tissue paper, Lillian selected a classic black cocktail purse.

"Mom," yelled Dan. "Hurry! We gotta go. Adam called. Peggy's at the church."

Back in her room, hopping into shoes, Lillian muttered more curses. *Dammit, of all days to be late!* She dumped out the contents of her mother's elegant framed bag. Oh, how her mother hung onto memorabilia. The yellow of an antique postcard contrasted against the pale blue bedspread. She picked it up. "OAK TREE. Basking Ridge, NJ 1944" There were no other words, no mailing address. Nothing to indicate why her mother saved it.

"Mom!" yelled Dan. "Now!"

She tucked the card back in the purse. Dan loved trees, timbered them for a living, maybe he would know what this meant. Hustling into the car, she kept the window down. "I'm a little over heated from all the exertion. I hate to be rushed," she said to Dan, implication in her tone.

Dan only smiled.

Leaves were beginning to turn. A crisp, October breeze promised glorious weather for the afternoon. An absolutely gorgeous day for her grandson to get married.

Pulling into the parking lot of the wedding venue, a repurposed farm, Lillian noticed her two granddaughters Katie and Lindsey fixing their hair and makeup using a pickup truck side mirror. "Hello girls," Lillian said. "What an exciting day and both of you look amazing as always," exclaimed Lillian. After Lillian exited the car, the girls responded with a hug and saying thank you Gram. "We'll see you Gram after the wedding ceremony," Katie & Lindsey stated in unison. At the reception, Lillian pulled out the postcard. "Dan, did you ever give grandma a tree postcard?" She handed the picture card to him.

"Hey, where did you get this? It's from 1944." Dan pointed to the tiny copyright at the bottom back of the card.

"It was stuck in her purse. I don't know how she got it. She's never been to Basking Ridge. I don't think she ever went to New Jersey except maybe to Atlantic City for the beach in the summer and that would have been year's ago." stated Lillian to Dan.

Adam and Peggy came up to Dan and his mother, hugging them. The newlyweds were glowing from happiness and a dozen or so champagne toasts. Lillian showed her grandson the postcard.

Adam froze and shot a glance at his father. "Uh yeah, nice tree."

"Isn't it huge?" Lillian said. "I don't know how mom would have gotten this, she never mentioned it."

"I wonder if it's still there," Peggy said. "What do you think Adam?"

Adam shrugged. "I don't know, maybe?"

"We should all go and see it," announced Lillian. "All of us, go and visit it. Well, em, after the honeymoon." She nudged Peggy playfully.

Peggy giggled. "Hey, let's you and me get some champagne!" She linked her arm into Lillian's and the two women skipped toward the bar.

"Uh, Dad?" Adam whispered. He nodded towards Lillian. "That tree, isn't that the one you're going to be taking down?"

1763

His legs were knotting in overuse. A half day-old spring sun beat down on his back. Time to rest. Thirsty, he fell to his knees at the bank of a small stream. Gulping a few handfuls of water, he looked up and sniffed the air. A whiff of decay. A swamp nearby? Maybe brackish water? Was he that close to the sea?

He crossed the stream. Sloshing through the shallow riffle, he paused and watched a tiny stain of disturbed sediment slip downstream. It was a good place to cross, they couldn't follow his tracks on rocks. The bank's soft mud would, however, hold the prints of his shoeless feet for hours. He continued through the stream, crawled up the tree roots along the water's edge. He turned, with the exception of the occasional staccato tat-tat-tat of a woodpecker, there was no sound. He carefully trotted over acres of cleared furrowed fields. Looking left and right, he slithered through a feeble tree line and spied a road. And still, no people. This was a gift. And he was not about to ignore it.

He glanced over his shoulder. Not a soul behind him.

Yet.

And then he saw shade, blessed, quiet shade.

Jeremy Tilridge, infantryman, Army of Regulars, 2nd brigade, leaned against a massive white oak. Its branches sprawled out low above the ground. Cool air shifted through barely budded lime green leaves.

"You're a good 'un, aren't ya?" He said to the tree. An odd tingle crept through his arm. *Was it me or did the tree flinch at my touch?* He rubbed the bark vigorously, under his hand, the rough surface grew warm.

The oak was in the process of overtaking a cemetery next to a small church (of course). Unlucky gravestones tilted, nosed off-plumb by the tree's equally sprawling roots. He wondered how long it would take to upheave the whole graveyard.

Jeremy wedged his body between a divot of trunk and collar root. He rubbed his blistered feet. A cloud rolled over the sun and the church's glass windows flashed light and dark. Jeremy noted the building's wooden log sides shimmered deep brown with freshly applied pitch. He leaned his head back. *What did I just do?*

On the second skirmish of the day against the savage butchers, he watched a man lose his brains. The musket ball hit the man's forehead. Jeremy heard a snap and the *crack-whoosh* as the entire contents of the man's skull emptied out the back of his shattered head. The man staggered and fell. Jeremy tightened his eyes and gulped to keep his gore down.

I'm next, he thought. *No, I'm not waiting to have my blood all over the ground.*

Ever so slowly, he crawled under the brush of rhododendron and along the floor of the woods, listening and listening. The French were pushing the entire British regiment back to the river. There wasn't much anyone could do it seemed.

A string of useless cannons of the 8th brigade sat on a ridge overlooking the Delaware aiming at nothing while he and his comrades were being picked off head by head. He stopped to listen. There wasn't a whisper, not as much as the snap of a twig. Ahead, a grove of black walnuts opened into a marshy meadow flanked by another stand of trees. All he needed to do was to get out of the line of fire and meet up with the rest of his group. *If there are any left.* He checked his powder bag and groaned. *Ah bloody hell, out of powder?* He should have stayed and taken the powder and balls from the fallen man. But he didn't have the stomach to dig about in a dead persons' things.

Then a shout, "*C'est la!*"

They spotted me! By pure primal instinct, Jeremy fled.

"I didn't mean it," he told the tree. He ran his hand through his sandy curls. "I just ran. The French were running too, falling all over each other. Never caught me, though, I was too fast." Fear had given Jeremy's feet wings. And before he knew it, he was past the point of return. Going back now to catch up with his fellow soldiers was foolishness. He wondered how far he was from his small homestead. Maybe several miles—a day's walk. Maybe a day's ride? Maybe nowhere near, but he felt close. Just his luck, so close and he had no way of getting back to Sarah.

The ugly label of "deserter" flitted through his mind. *Either way, I'm a dead man. Either way, I get shot.* He hung his head and wept for his pregnant wife. He cried for all the promises he'd made to her, now unable to keep. She'd be waiting for his return. No one would tell her. He'd never be able to let her know what happened.

"Damn this whole thing!" he shouted. A strong breeze blew through the tree. Its leaves rustled to erase the curse from the sacred space. Jeremy sobbed louder.

"There he is!"

This time he understood the English. He smiled in recognition. *A friendly,* he thought, but his relief was short lived.

Jeremy didn't recognize the commander. Introduced as Captain Harold Jensen, the new captain of the reformulated 2nd brigade, the Captain didn't recognize Jeremy. He whirled about on a lathered horse and barked questions as to why Jeremy was unshod and three miles from the *rendezvous* point. Jeremy pleaded his case. Truly, he had not seen a living man from his brigade. Only a few of the faces of the seven or so men who gathered before Jeremy were familiar. None of them were witnesses to his original situation, his only defense was his word. "I know I ran but I was just going back to my pregnant—," Jeremy's words were cut short.

"Therefore, this man is a deserter," the commander pronounced. "Shoot him."

"Nah!" George MacIlwain stepped forward. "Jeremy Tilridge wouldna do such a thing."

"That's right," agreed Benjamin White. "Captain Jensen, I beg you…"

"I said, shoot him!"

Jeremy backed up against the tree. "Georgie, Benny, help me."

Frozen to the ground, the men only exchanged glances.

"Oh god, you cowards," Captain Jensen yelled. He pulled out his loaded Queen Anne and shot Jeremy.

The young man and the tree were instantly forged together, sharing lead, as the musket ball exited one and entered the other.

George and Benjamin lurched forward to grab Jeremy. But it was too late. His body sank to the base of the tree.

"Back to your line," Captain Jensen ordered.

"Ya dinnae hafta do that," George stormed.

"Shall I shoot you too?"

"Go on, do it," challenged Benjamin. "And shoot me too, right in front of all your men. That will get you tossed right quick."

Captain Jensen remained silent.

"We canna leave this body a'this." George ran his hands through his hair. "A blessed church ta boot. It's unholy to let 'em lay thus."

"He's a traitor," snapped Captain Jensen.

"Only God knows what he is now." Benjamin's tone was low and level. The truth made Captain Jensen look away.

"Captain, we're a' Jock Tamson's bairns," he said. "Jerm'y needs a buryin'."

"Bury him then," Captain Jensen growled. "Just do it. And do it quickly."

The men all helped dig a shallow grave with their bayonets for Jeremy Tilridge, infantryman, Army of Regulars, 2nd brigade. They placed the body in a space shaded by the tree's largest branch. Some sniffled while a few prayers were said.

"You're a lucky man, Jeremy," muttered Benjamin to the mound of dirt. "We're going back into the hellfire soon."

One of the men found a piece of shale and scratched out a marker, misspelling the name. "Was he married?" asked the soldier. "Maybe put 'husband' under his name?"

"Oh no," Benjamin sighed, recalling Jeremy speak of his wife, Sarah. "She's the prettiest creature I ever seen, Bennie," Jeremy had said. "We're expecting our first. Can't wait 'til we get back."

"Who's gonna tell her?" George's question hung in the air.

"Can we let his wife know?" Benjamin looked around. "Their farm isn't too far from here. She's with child." For a moment Benjamin thought he had pushed his luck too far.

"Only if it is on the way to our rendezvous point, then we will inform her." Captain Jensen conceded, wriggled in his saddle, but never got off his horse.

As they trudged south towards the Tilridge Farm, the men talked, grew silent and then talked again as if each were fighting an emotional battle; taking the hills, losing the valleys. Benjamin knew they were as hungry and exhausted as he was. And every one of them, down to the last man, held no ill thing against Jeremy. *Bad enough to watch a madman shoot a good soldier, now that same madman is off to tell the man's widow.* Benjamin thought, *it's enough to make a body quit the army.* He dreaded telling the woman, who Jeremy described as having blue eyes as bold as a January sky.

Every now and again Benjamin stole a glance at Captain Jensen. He looked grim, clenched-jaw and white as a bone.

CHAPTER THREE

The tree of liberty must be refreshed from time to time with the blood of patriots and tyrants.
--Thomas Jefferson, letter to William
Stephens Smith (John Adams' son-in-law), 1787

The teen gripped the steering wheel, eyes focused straight ahead. His companion noticed the white knuckles on his friend's hands and laughed, "Don't be such a chicken shit, Justin."

"I'm not a chicken shit," Justin protested. He loosened his grip on the wheel. His braces were killing him tonight. Two more weeks and they're off.

"Com'on we gotta get to the cemetery before Midnight," Greg urged his friend. "You lost a bet, now you gotta do this." Greg pulled out his iPhone. "And I'm gonna record you screaming like a little girl."

Justin hung his head, sighed and put the car in drive. Why now? Any other time—spring, summer or even winter—he'd be perfectly fine with a cemetery dare. But freakin' October and Halloween was this weekend. As he approached the church, overpowered by the large oak, he turned the car right and down the small road that ran the length of the cemetery. It seemed darker than normal. The church's motion lights weren't working and the area was unlit. Making matters worse, his car's headlights were accentuating cemetery shadows against the south side of the church. Justin parked the car on the side road. He retrieved a mini-LED flashlight from the console and flicked it a few times.

"Here we go." Greg was gleeful. He tapped the phone screen and began to narrate. "This is the story of a stupid idiot who took a dare to sit in a graveyard for five minutes after midnight."

"Shut up, Greg," Justin groaned. "Can you knock it off and help me find the right marker?"

Greg cackled, but acquiesced. He used the phone's torch app to light the way. The teens crept along the uneven rows of markers and searched the headstones.

"Who are we looking for again?" asked Greg.

"WHO??!! What are you? An owl? We are looking for Tilridge, a soldier of the French and Indian War (Seven Year War) who was shot while resting under an oak tree. The very oak tree that we are standing under now. This old oak was known to the early American Indians of this area as the Great Oak Tree that sang and shared its Spirit with those who touched it and respected it. So when the bullet went through Tilridge's skull and into the tree, the soldier and the tree became one. Since then, the Spirit of the Great Oak Tree can be heard singing and sighing when the wind blows through its branches even without touching it. The sounds and Spirit of the Great Oak Tree, so the legend goes, inspires people to write songs and music while relaxing under it. Musical instruments made from a fallen limb also have a unique sound. The name is "Jeremy Tilridge" but anything close is fine since it may have been misspelled," replied Justin.

A light breeze kicked up and flitted through the Great Oak Tree. Its leaves rattled a warning to the boys. Instinctively, Justin looked up and to his dismay, only a sliver of a moon was visible through the Oak's battered, nearly leafless branches. He picked his way carefully through the maze of slate, granite and marble gravestones. Finding no name matching either "Jeremy" or "Tilridge," Justin returned to the beginning of the next row.

"I can't read half of these, it's like a different language," complained Greg. "Maybe we're in the wrong place."

"It's mostly German because it was founded by a—,"

"A what?"

Justin froze. He pointed to a mist that floated ever so slowly around the north side of the church and swam through the cemetery. It settled in a particularly dense manner around one stone. Justin, hand shaking, shone his small LED light on the dull slate slab. Both he and Greg could just make out the letters, T-I-L-L-R-I-D. Once illuminated, the mist unfurled from around the grave marker and seeped toward the two.

Greg and Justin exchanged glances.

"Run!"

The next day, Dan pointed to black tire marks on the road. "Looks like someone needed to get out of here in a hurry."

Adam laughed. "Somebody either didn't want to get caught or was being chased."

"Well careful you don't trip over any broken beer bottles," said Dan as he beeped his truck lock.

"I don't think so Dad, this town isn't known for crazy parties."

"And how would you know?"

Adam shrugged. "I'm in the loop. I hear things," he playfully punched his father. "We can check with Officer Hank and ask if he had any calls last night and Dad, thanks for bringing me along."

"No problem. Let's take a walk around, Ken and Gilly should be here any minute."

"Have you told Gran about the tree coming down?"

Dan shook his head. "I need to really have a sit-down with her. She's doing some insane family tree research. Like Genealogy 101. She can't get that postcard out of her mind."

"Can you blame her? It's like an unsolved mystery."

The two men walked around the tree. Its roots, bold and bare, were as impressive as its branches. The soil was disappearing and the cemetery headstones leaned drunkenly, helpless to thwart the powerful surge of the tree's growth. Adam stubbed his foot on a smaller exposed root and braced himself against an aged slab of slate.

"Hey, what's this?" He bent to pick up a shiny black cylinder.

Dan took the mini-LED flashlight from Adam's hand. "Huh, I guess someone from the church dropped it." He pocketed the light and made a mental note to reach out to Pastor Tom about their find.

"Dad, I think you should get Gram here before the tree comes down."

"Oh, don't worry, I will."

"I mean what if one of our ancestors is buried here?" Adam gestured to the cemetery.

"Not a chance," said Dan, resolute.

1763

Sarah Tilridge stood up and dropped her hoe. She massaged the small of her back and ran through the dates in her head. This baby would be born in the fall, an unfortunate time. Babies born in the harvest time took attention from preparations for winter. Winters here were unhappy, with snow so deep you forgot where the wood pile was. What awful timing.

She hoped Jeremy would be back soon to re-dig the root cellar. It collapsed under the weight of the melting snow. The split rail was rotting near the corner of the pasture. And the roof had started to leak. She patched it as best she could. "Was there a blessed thing that wasn't falling down on this farm?" Sarah muttered as the sun heated her fair hair.

Oh lud, forgot my bonnet.

She'd been so forgetful lately. She blamed it on the pregnancy. And her night terrors on the pregnancy as well. Though she knew better, even as a little girl, her occasional bad dreams were dire warnings. She had forecasted a horse going lame and indeed it happened. When she told her mother Uncle Peter wasn't coming to visit because she dreamt he was sick with fever, she was told to hush. Did her mother think she was some sort of witch? But Uncle Peter never came. From then on, her mother said, "Hush, but heed your evil dreams." Last night, she dreamed Jeremy had a horrible fever and blood was coming from his mouth. She awoke with a scream, the baby in her womb jumped too.

She heard the men before she saw them. The sounds of a cart rattle, a snorting horse and the trudging footsteps of a group of men, which would normally cheer her heart but now caused concern. Were they French?

Sarah met them on the path, happy to recognize their uniforms as regulars. "Tell me why you're all here?" No one looked happy to see her. She steadied herself against a fence post. "Where's Jeremy?"

"I'm sorry ma'am, I have to--," Captain Jensen gasped. He said nothing more.

All eyes turned. Jensen was swaying in his saddle. He began to list to one side. The men caught him before he fell to the ground.

Sarah gingerly touched Jensen's boot; blood glistened in strands from his calf to below his ankle. Some blood had congealed on the leather mixing with the mud already caked there.

"Ack," yelled George, "he's a sore wounded!"

Jensen was barely conscious, mumbling that they should keep moving. Demanding to know why they had stopped. He kept repeating the word "insubordination." One of the men looked at Sarah. "Is he dying?"

"Get him into the house," Sarah ordered.

"Yes, ma'am." Benjamin and George hauled Jensen off his horse and half-carried, half-dragged him up the path and into the small wooden structure. They laid him on a pallet in front of the meager fireplace.

Sarah propped up Jensen's head and asked Benjamin to pry off Jensen's boot. With great care, he pulled off the boot, eliciting groans from Jensen.

She had George rip strips for bandages from an old muslin sheet. After cleaning out Jensen's wound, Sarah packed herbs into a plaster, soaked it with milk and linseed oil, than applied it to his leg. "This is going to need some stitching maybe." The gash was deep and had gone through boot leather and skin.

George and Benjamin stayed near the unconscious man. The rest of the men huddled outside the doorway, helpless.

"Do they have anything to eat?" Sarah asked. Sighing, "Look at them, they are like lost sheep."

"No ma'am," said Benjamin. "Nothing for a day now."

She directed the men to the dammed-up pool that Jeremy had made after the winter thaw. "Catch anything that's swimming," she said. "Look sharp, them ground grouse have been laying for a bit." She pointed to the meadow behind the house. "And if you're good enough with a call and a sling, there's a gobbler with his flock." She halted the two men before they moved. "Not one shot, lest you want to bring the savages down upon us."

George cupped and hawked a male gobbler call. While it sounded awful to Benjamin, it was enough to pique the interest of the male gobbler as Sarah predicted. The male, perceiving a threat, got a little too close to George. A rain of small accurate rocks stunned the bird and George was on him, knife flashing.

That evening, the men feasted on small trout, boiled grouse eggs, turkey and an onion broth that Sarah made with the fat drippings from the thin gobbler.

Sarah inspected Jensen's wound. She wasn't a surgeon, but being handy with a needle, she was able to stitch together some of the torn muscle and skin. She shook her head. "I've seen old blankets with better edges than this." At least the wound was closed. She tied fresh bandages dipped in linseed oil around his leg. If it was a deep infection, her time had just been wasted.

"He'll probably be swelled and sore now," she told Benjamin. "Can't promise that he'll be able to ride a horse any time soon."

"Thank you so much. You've done more than any one—the Captain's lucky to be alive."

"I don't know if he will be tomorrow," she admitted.

George and Benjamin stayed inside the small hut. The rest of the men pitched tents and remained outside. Snores wafted through the window. Although his skin glistened with sweat in the firelight, Jensen's breathing was regular and deep.

Benjamin pulled Sarah aside and in low tones, gave her the unofficial explanation of Jeremy's death. He didn't exaggerate but indicated that Jeremy's death was unwarranted. Her reaction surprised him. He expected Sarah to sob and fret, but she only sighed. She stood up and looked out the papered window.

"Guess I'll have to re-dig the root cellar," she whispered. "How can I keep this place?" She'd never been so close to despair. "Not sure if I can even find an unbroken shovel."

"Do you have relatives nearby? Maybe you should go back home," advised Benjamin.

"No, I'm here and the fields are started. A neighbor up the stream a-ways, stops in from time to time. I hoped Jeremy, well, he's gone now." She sighed deeply. "I can't stay neither."

They stared into the fire, listened to the crackling. It should have felt safe and secure, tonight the crackling sounded hollow and nothing seemed safe and secure.

"Take me with you?" She spoke to the fire. "I have no one to help me tend the farm." She hugged her belly. "This one's coming in the fall," she said. "Not sure how I'll manage."

Both men were unable to offer any comforting words.

Not waiting for an answer, she rubbed at her eyes and curled up in a chair, not caring what tomorrow would bring. If the baby be a boy, she decided she'd name him Jeremy Jr.

By morning, Jensen was lucid, groggy but aware of his surroundings. He was appraised of his situation, of the widow who sewed his leg wound, tended his fever, fed his men and allowed his horse to graze on her land. They also told him of her strength and matter-of-fact acceptance of her husband's death and her new, unanticipated situation. With each word, Jensen's heart cracked considerably deeper.

"I need to do right by this woman," he croaked, throat dry. "I have no money, no supplies, nothing to remedy this situation." His hoarse voice betrayed some emotion. His pride in tatters. He had nothing to repay the gold of Christian charity.

Benjamin frowned. "Well sir, she needs something more than money."

"Ah, she needs someone to help her," explained George. "I can—," he began.

"No." Jensen was adamant. "I can't spare you. I had orders. We were to engage the enemy at a specific rendezvous," he gritted through his teeth as he tried to stand. Then he hissed in pain and sunk back down.

"What can you do?" Benjamin prodded. "Can't you do something for her?"

Jensen shook his head. "I do not know. I've only know that I have taken from her the very thing that would sustain her." He looked desolate. "I didn't kill one person, I've killed three."

"Enough." Benjamin stood up, "You remain. We'll return to that small town, see if there's anything, anyone—maybe there's news."

"Aye, let us go back," agreed George. "Yer wound tisn't letting you go a'wheres."

"I don't think it's wise," Jensen protested. But Benjamin and George persisted. Jensen was to stay with a group of three men, while the rest of them returned to the town, seeking news and perhaps help.

"No more than a two day's trip," Benjamin promised. Jensen informally gave him a second-in-command rank.

Sarah watched them leave and as the sun sank lower, she tried to focus on the future. The noises of the remaining men—some laughter here and there—felt oddly comforting. Small solace for a lost husband.

She had been counting on Jeremy's return. This was their life and it was supposed to be lived together. "We'll go to the northern colonies," he said. "We'll settle where we can get land for pennies and have our own farm. Our own life, in a new land." Sarah wasn't so sure. She had heard stories about the savages in the new land. They fascinated and frightened her, these people of different colors and exotic dress.

But it sounded so good the way he said it. Sounded so easy and pretty. She was done at home, tired of fighting with her siblings. Her prospects were bleak in County Cork. Without money or title, there was little else to do other than to die in poverty.

She married Jeremy in a simple wedding. Her mother said they made an odd pair. Jeremy with his brown cow-eyes and sunny smile contrasted with Sarah's white-blond hair and clear blue eyes and sad face. "I don't need your mean bits, ma," said Sarah. "I need your prayers." Her mother had sniffed at the request. Sarah packed a small chest of all her belongings and left the village. She didn't look back.

Less than a week later, she and Jeremy found themselves on a ship to the new colonies. Jeremy had hired them off as coupled indentured servants—so they'd be purchased together. He promised Sarah their seven years would go by quickly. The death of the indenturing agent during the voyage was the only blessing they'd received. Unable to honor or negate their indenture, the solicitor handed them the writ and deed to the land. He confided to them, it was easily flooded and nestled in between a river and a huge swamp. "Still, it's all yours," he told them and folded a map inside the deed.

They left Philadelphia, heading north along the Delaware River, seeing more trees than people. At Reading's Ferry, they turned east. A day's journey later, they found their parcel of land to be in tillable shape, cleared well by prior tenants. A small log dugout, enhanced by Jeremy's capable hands, became their home.

But when the first snowflakes fell, so did their luck. No sooner had Sarah informed him that she was pregnant than word came that the French were marching from the north into the region just west of the Delaware. Had they settled in the wrong place and now needed to move? Would she give birth, only to have angry French soldiers descend upon them?

Jeremy assured her the war was a mere land dispute and, "much too west of here for us to be worried," he added.

However, he enlisted in the Provincial troops. They needed to buy livestock and the bounties promised by the governor for enlisting were too good to pass up. Again, Jeremy soothed her worries by telling her, he'd only been recruited for one campaign season. "It won't last long, don't worry, I'll probably never shoot my rifle," he laughed. "Well it didn't last long for you Jeremy," Sarah said out loud without thinking. The sound of her voice caused Captain Jensen to wake from a sound nap.

Captain Jensen noticed that Sarah was silently crying. He didn't know how to comfort her so he thanked her for tending to his wound. He told her that he should be well enough to ride when the other soldiers returned in two days as promised by Benjamin.

Meanwhile the way back to town felt slower for Benjamin and George. The two men arrived at the large oak. The blood stain, still noticeable had turned brown. They took notice of the rocks laid atop Jeremy's grave. "Well, the grave site will be obvious and easy to remember being next to this large oak tree," remarked Benjamin.

"Shuddna happened," George shook his head. The church bells rang--Midday.

Benjamin ordered the men to find a councilor-at-large or mayor. "A town official of some sort," he told the men. "We need to report and regroup should there be another brigade nearby." He and George were to search the northeast section and the rest of the men were to search the southwest part of town.

A few moments later, Benjamin spied a group of horses heading towards the church. George cried, "Oh aye, a'look, militia." Benjamin ordered George to gather the rest of the men and meet back at the oak tree.

As Benjamin approached the militia, he stopped in his tracks. Leading the group of soldiers was Colonel Washington. When Benjamin drew closer to the group, Colonel Washington ordered him to halt and identify himself. Benjamin White infantryman, Army of Regulars, 2nd brigade, Sir. "Where is your Captain?" demanded Colonel Washington. "He is injured and is recovering at a farm near here," replied Benjamin. George and the rest of the men had returned to the tree while Benjamin was responding to Colonel Washington. Unable to control his emotions even in the presence of the Colonel, George relayed the story of Jeremy and the wounded Captain Harold Jensen. How the Captain shot Jeremy Tilridge and then how Jeremy's pregnant wife saved the Captain life. And how she also fed the troop and provided shelter for them. "Mrs. Tilridge should be compensated for her service, Sir," blurted George. Benjamin added, "The Captain wishes to do right by her, Sir."

Colonel Washington was moved by the account and knew full well the challenges Mrs. Tilridge would face. Without hesitation Colonel Washington gave orders to Benjamin and George to find a female servant or slave for Mrs. Tilridge along with food supplies and a cow.

Benjamin being pleased with the order said, "Yes Sir, and what should I tell Captain Jensen?" "Tell him that his orders have changed," Colonel Washington stated. The Colonel returned to his horse, withdrew several papers from his saddle bag, wrote on the documents, conferred with his Second in Command and nodded to Benjamin saying, "Here, give these documents to Captain Jensen. They will address any questions he may have about his new orders and about the plan to repay Mrs. Tilridge for her unselfish service to him and his soldiers. "

"Yes Sir, thank you."

Colonel Washington saluted and the soldiers returned his salute.

Benjamin, George and the other infantrymen did as ordered. They purchased a young female salve at Reading's Ferry, bought a cow and food supplies using the money provided by Colonel Washington.

When they returned to the Tilridge farm with their purchases, they found Captain Jensen up and about and the soldiers left with him were patching the dugout's roof.

Benjamin drew Captain Jensen to the side and told him about meeting up with Colonel Washington at the Great Oak Tree where Jeremy was sh......buried. Realizing the great sorrow the Captain now felt, Benjamin quickly handed the Captain the documents from Colonel Washington. Captain Jensen recognized Colonel Washington's signature and was pleased with his new orders. Jensen and his men were to head west to the Delaware and reunite with the 3rd brigade.

The next morning Captain Jensen gathered his men to depart from the widow's farm. He parted a different man as though the fever burned away his arrogance. After bestowing food supplies, a thin cow and a young female servant to Sarah,

Jensen took his leave. He even kissed Sarah's hand. She blushed to the roots of her hair.

The men waved goodbye.

"Do you think she'll survive?" asked Benjamin.

Captain Jensen nodded. "If anyone can survive, it's that woman."

CHAPTER FOUR

And silence through the trees did run:
They asked no question as I went --They stood too high for
astonishment --
They could see God sit on His throne.
-- Elizabeth Barrett Browning, The Runaway Slave at Pilgrim's Point

Dan and Adam conducted informal measurements. The numbers, though Dan knew them by heart, still astounded him. Adam logged the basic stats and read them aloud.

"So, rounded measurements here," he reported to his father. "We've got a circumference of 18.4 feet and a diameter of 9.3."

Dan nodded. "Height?"

"My drone read 102 feet even. Ken and Gilly's measurement was just a hair shorter."

Dan had seen the images. They showed branches which stretched to an incredible width. He had never encountered a tree that had a drip line over 100 feet. Images also showed a cobweb of cables holding branches with enough tension to let them sway but not snap. It also provided the most disheartening images of unrelenting decay. There were numerous holes from boring insects and pockmarked bark where it was clear woodpeckers and sapsuckers regularly dined on the oak. There were two scorch scars where the tree was struck by lightning.

"Hey, here you go." Adam handed Dan an acorn.

"Stop picking stuff up, will ya?"

"Doesn't seem to be too many around here though," Adam noted.

"It's not a masting year, you know when it just carpets the ground with acorns, and she's," Dan paused. "She's dying.

"She?"

"Yep she, as in, Martha." Dan pointed to a tiny headstone that was lovingly embraced by the tree's root. The last name was eroded by time and weather but the first name Martha was still legible. "I think the tree picked its own name. It was probably a little kid."

"How do you know?"

Dan shrugged. "I don't, but small stone, small person."

Adam stepped gingerly over the headstone.

"Don't worry, they moved the bodies a while back." Dan waved to the west side of the church. "They're safe there."

"So, Martha is going to die?"

"Martha is dying, if not already dead. She's unsafe and as much as I'd love to keep her going, I can't. But we'll see what Ken and Gilly say. But I guarantee you they're not going to want to deliver the bad news."

"Thought you said that Pastor Tom was thinking it was time to take it down."

"Yeah, but…"

Adam halted his father in mid-sentence. "Hold on, we're being watched."

"How about that." Dan smiled. "I bet I know who lost this flashlight." He patted his front pocket.

Justin and Greg were sitting on a bench in front of the Washington House. Chatter from patrons on the outside patio enjoying coffee and croissants grated on Justin's nerves. Too many people! The two boys studied the actions of the two men with a concentration that rivaled any surveillance team.

Justin chewed his lip. "We have to go back and pick up the light."

"Okay, so let's go."

"How many times do I have to tell you? We have to wait 'til those guys leave."

"Oh, com'on just go over and get it."

"No, I don't want them asking any questions."

"Then go buy a new light."

"It's my Dad's, he'll know," Justin's voice cracked.

Greg stood up. "I'm done. We either go now or I leave, okay?" Just then Officer Hank walked up to the boys and put a hand on each of the boy's shoulder and asked, "Is everything okay boys?" "Yes, we are fine Officer Hank. We just need to talk to the tree guys," replied Greg. Justin thanked Officer Hank for his concern and added, "We'll see you in school on Monday." Justin rubbed his face and said, "Alright, let go see the tree guys." The boys crossed the street" It took a lot of courage along with prodding from Greg for Justin to say hello and tell the men he had lost a flashlight. As Dan listened to Justin, he looked over Adam's shoulder and gave a thumbs up to Officer Hank as he walked by them.

Dan smiled. "I figured that was why you came." "Here you go." He handed over the flashlight. The look on Justin's face was pure relief. "What were you doing here?" Dan inquired.

"Ah, I'm working on a history project," Justin lied.

Greg barely squelched a laugh.

"Yeah? You learning local history?"

Justin nodded. "Yep. And I found out, it's an old cemetery and the tree is maybe like, 200 or 250 years old."

Dan laughed. "This girl?" He patted Martha's bark. "No, she's easily around 500 to 600."

"Years?" Justin and Greg's jaws both popped open.

"How can you possibly know that?" Greg demanded. "It's not like you can count the rings or anything."

"Not yet," Adam murmured.

"Oh!" Justin exclaimed. "You're the guys knocking the tree down!"

"Not exactly." Dan explained that technically Adam was along for support, but there would be an entire team of qualified people involved to remove the tree. He didn't have to ask how the kids knew the tree was to be taken down. In a small town like Basking Ridge, secrets weren't guarded too carefully. He also told the kids it wasn't as easy as just taking a chain saw and slicing the tree at its base and yelling, "Timber!" All anyone had to do was to, "Look up," he said. "You can see the cables, connections and even the decay." That, he informed the boys, made it essential to take the tree down slowly, carefully, branch by branch.

"Are you going to have to move the graveyard?" Justin asked, glancing over at the headstone. "What if something falls on the stones?"

"Not to worry. They're safe, besides, the bodies were already moved," Dan was puzzled. "You guys are locals. Didn't you know?"

Greg snickered and Justin punched him on the arm. "You liar, you said everything was still here!"

"Hey, it doesn't matter," Greg laughed, rubbing his arm. "Besides it doesn't explain the mist."

"Mist?" asked Dan.

Justin smacked a hand to his face. "Nice job, big mouth."

"Yeah, we saw it the other night," Greg began, undaunted by the glares sent his way from Justin. "Jerk face here, lost a bet and had to come to the Tilridge headstone and sit there at midnight for five minutes. But there was a mist and he ran."

"Uh, you're the jerk face, we both ran," Justin corrected.

"Wait, did you say 'Tilridge'?" Dan asked. "That's a familiar-sounding name."

"Dad, wait a second," Adam began.

"That's great granddad's name," Dan said snapping his fingers.

1763

The young female slave was bright, though her English was hardly understandable. Sarah took her in happily, though she hated the idea of having a slave. Her consolation was that the slave was like her, free, albeit by a peculiarity. She taught her the best English she could. And the girl took to each task with an energy that gave Sarah hope for her farm's success. The only drawback was that the girl was too different and spooked so easily.

One day, the girl knocked over a small clay bowl. Rather than picking up the pieces, she ran and hid in the corner cowering. Shaking her head and begging Sarah not to whip her. "Please don't," she cried. I not a-mean to break it!"

Sarah was shocked, she'd never beaten anything, not even a stray dog.

"Listen to me," she grasped the girl's hands. "Don't carry on so." She patted her on the head. It felt an odd, motherly gesture toward someone not much younger than she. "Let me tell you now, you are my help, not my slave." Sarah shook her head. "Not a slave, understand?"

The girl wiped her eyes with her sleeve and nodded her head.

"I can't own a body. I never so a-thinking like that."

The girl nodded again.

"I can't be beating you," Sarah said. "You can't get work from a dead mule, now can you?"

The girl shook her head.

"I only need for you to not to be afraid. Oh lud, when the baby comes, you may have to do a lot of the work by yourself."

The girl nodded again.

"I can't call you 'girl' while we're living here," Sarah said. "So, do you have a name? What do I call you?"

The girl thought for a moment. "Oh, I like your name, Sarah Tilridge." The girl smiled. "I can be Sarah too!"

For the first time in a long time, Sarah laughed. "No, we can't both be Sarah."

"Til-ridge? I can be Tilridge."

"No that's not right either."

"Till? Rid? Tilly?"

"Well, there you be, Tilly Tilridge."

One late summer afternoon, still, humid air hung over the women plucking corn. Sweat dripped down their backs as they pried and pulled the sweet ears off their stalks. These were the days Sarah could smell the muck and mire of the large swamp due east. She'd never ventured to see it. "Smells of dead things," she told Tilly. A cool wind from the west whipped through the corn rows. Sarah looked up. Huge thunderheads rolled above their heads.

"Storm's a'coming," Tilly warned.

Sarah stretched and rubbed her neck. "You go back to the house, I need to finish my row," she breathed. Near her time, she waddled over to empty her basket into Tilly's. "I'll be along shortly."

Tilly nodded. "Don't be too long."

A boom echoed over their heads. Followed by a crack and a zigzag of lightning. Tilly hustled back to house and Sarah pulled at the corns in earnest. It'll rain soon. I can stand a little wet. But the rain didn't come. Wind increased in ferocity and the booms and cracks increased in violence. One boom exploded so close to Sarah, it knocked her off her feet. Lightning flashed followed by a deafening crack. Blinded for a moment, Sarah struggled to her feet. She blinked hard and staggered down the corn row.

The smell of smoke jerked her head up. Something's on fire? Sarah grabbed a stalk for support. The wind was fanning flames from ignited hay at the end of the corn field. It was headed directly toward her. Sarah spun around but lost her footing and hit the ground. She saved her belly by landing on her hip. The flames were chewing at her skirt. Before she could cry out for help, Tilly was on top of her, beating down the flames and putting them out with her bare hands. She dragged Sarah out of the corn row and the two women coughed and retched until they reached the house.

Thank you, Sarah gasped. She touched Tilly's face. "You saved my life."

Tilly nodded. "I ain't a slave no more."

They returned to the field the next morning. They saved some of the corn, hoed over the scorched stalks and covered over the field with the remainder of the burned hay. The contrast between the two couldn't have been starker. Sarah blond and fair, Tilly with dusky dark skin. At first glance, the two were slave and owner. But if a passerby listened closely to their conversation, they talked as a pair of friends born far away now catching up on all the goings-on. The women worked hard side-by-side, blessed with supplies and tools gifts from Colonel Washington and Captain Jensen. Sarah and Tilly managed a respectable harvest without Jeremy.

They managed to protect a few meager chickens. Sarah taught Tilly how to shoot Jeremy's Brown Bess. She warned her to never shoot a body, just varmints going after chickens. Tilly was able to shoot at a fox, but it ran off before she could kill it. Sarah said it was for the best, it won't come back and you saved a musket ball for the next one. For two days the women dug in the upper fields. They packed the repaired root cellar with potatoes, turnips and carrots.

Sarah and Tilly did their best to stand watch over the chickens and root cellar to protect their source of food from animals and thieves. This was all they had for themselves. One evening, in early fall, Sarah's back began to ache. "Tilly I can't sit. I can't stand. Not feeling so well."

Tilly's eyes flew open wide. "It's your time, Sarah."

Twin boys arrived on a frosty morning in October. And their birthdate was the only thing that the two brothers shared.

Flailing and screaming Adam Wendell Tilridge came into the world trailed by the smaller, quieter, Jeremy Grant Tilridge Jr.

Luck now seemed to come in pairs of good and bad. Good luck was announced by an abundance of corn and beans that kindly folk brought to them as an act of charity. Bad luck followed by both the plow and shovel breaking on the same day. The women managed with help from a growing number of neighbors who settled a few miles on either side of the farm. Life was hard and quiet. Until the boys began to walk and talk.

One day, while the boys were gathering eggs, noise interrupted Tilly and Sarah's plans for the spring planting of the fields.

Adam and Jeremy had poked each other until Jeremey was scratched and bleeding. Naturally, he yelled for his mother. Adam laughed at the result, having attained what he considered a victory. Tilly swatted at the older twin. "No! You should be ashamed," she hissed at the boy. "You never make another person bleed!"

Sarah tended to Jeremy's injury and kissed his fair head. Jeremy Jr. was as opposite as he could be from his dark brown eyed brother Adam.

"The way those two carry on so, they are like Cain and Abel." Tilly remarked.

Sarah closed her eyes, and agreed silently. Indeed, so much like the Bible tale. And she knew how badly it ended.

When the boys were ten years old, they went to town. The little family made it their goal to walk into town to hear a special "freedom" speech under the Great Oak Tree. Like many towns in the colonies, which had trees known as "Freedom

Trees" where people gathered to share news and socialize. For Sarah it served as a chance to visit Jeremy's grave. And tend it, if needs be. The people at the church never minded that someone was buried there who had neither affiliation to the church nor family in its congregation. Sarah was certain church folk must have known about her husband dying as a deserter. For some reason, they rendered to his stone the same respect as any war veteran was awarded.

A neighbor had stopped to make the formal invitation to the speech and presentation. "We are to be a free and independent nation," he announced triumphantly.

"That's odd enough," Sarah said to Tilly after the man left. "We already are, aren't we?"

"Maybe this land will join to France?"

Sarah frowned. "We just fought a war against them and I thought we won." Both women were more afraid and confused then they had been in those early years when Jeremy had passed. They had nothing but a few chickens and meager provisions carefully stowed in the corners of the home.

The trip was something everyone anticipated with excitement. The boys were beside themselves. A trip into Basking Ridge was becoming more and more prominent in the fixture of the colonies. This was no annual trip into town. This was an event, and to the boys it meant food. And a lot of it. Treats they were not used to tasting. People they were not used to seeing. A delight for all the senses.

Under the Great Oak, Sarah found her husband's grave marker. She made the boys pray at the spot and they picked wild flowers to place over the soil. The boys were most impressed with the tree and saw the remnants of a rope. "What's that for?" asked little Jeremy Jr. Adam was jumping up to reach for the dangling shreds.

Sarah shuddered. There were rumors that a French spy was hung from one of the large branches of the tree. "I don't know," she answered and scooted the boys away.

From behind a larger gravestone, up popped Charles Rex Scruff, better known to the townsfolk as "Scruffy." Like a bright and sunny daisy, he unexpectedly appeared and began to sing and strum his rough-looking angel lute.

Sarah and Tilly started, but they boys moved closer to inspect the instrument. Scruffy had planed and finished a fallen oak branch from the Great Oak to supply the stiff and sturdy neck piece. A cigar box, pilfered from a gentleman at Widow White's Tavern formed the body of the instrument. Twin sets of horse hair strings, that when brushed over by Scruffy's fingers, made a remarkable sound. No other noise, neither animal nor man matched the instrument's voice. It was the most joyful sound the boys had ever heard. Sarah thought the result was as loud and as twangy as Scruffy's own voice. "What would you boys like to hear me sing?"

They only stared.

"Hmm, no favorites, I see," he said with a wink. "Well I'll sing one of me favorites for ya."

Oh, the thirsty fly sat upon my knee
"Give us sip, a sip," said he.
"Oh no sir!" I replied, "It cannot be."

"I must fly to sweet Betsy."
"I must fly to sweet Betsy."

Scruffy finished and gave his helpless audience a smile.

Sarah, struggled with a compliment and said, "Thank you, sir, but we have no pence to give you."

"Oh no, no. I wouldn't dream of taking a farthing from you."

"Why are you in a cemetery?" Adam asked.

"Well now, aren't you a bold little fella!" Scruff's smile widened. He bent low and whispered, "Because this is the only place no one tells me to leave." He threw his head back and laughed.

Sarah and Tilly pulled the boys away.

Sarah, Tilly and the boys went to the church to hear the Freedom Speech. The speech bored the boys to distraction, but the speech quite worried the women. The boys eventually scampered away to the back of the church where Scruffy held court.

Most of his impromptu audiences were children the boys' own age and older. With his twangy style, he spun happy tunes. But as the independence presentation concluded, Scruffy knew his audience would be gathered up. He saved the saddest tune for last. He showed children the black scar marring the southwest corner of the church. "Oh, the sad, sad story of the burned down church," he said, then strummed and sang, "I'll sing you the tale of this church, the tale of Pastor David's Little Lamb."

A pastor from old German land came to this place with wife in hand.
And aimed to settle here, here on this land.
They had ten children; ten children had he.
But his favorite of all, was his little girlie.
Her name was Agnes, a little lamb was she,
As sweet and gentle and fine as could be.
She was his reason to smile, his reason to hope.
Until the British came with bayonets and rope.
Ho, ho, said the pastor, if ye send me to heaven, I can thank ye.
But the cruel British soldier, the awful man, took David's little lamb.
"I'll not send thee to heaven but curse ye to hell!"
He cut the fair little one and her blood did spill.
Oh! Cried the pastor, his little one run through, despaired his heart and with rage anew,
Set about to burn all 'til they withdrew.
Alas, what a burnin' bloody muddle over a slain little lamb,
Whose heart had wrapped 'round the pastor's, the pastor, now damned.

Tilly and Sarah walked home in silence trying to grapple with all the words spoken by the speakers about freedom and comments by the crowd. Any talk of a revolution with the British seemed terrifying. But the horror stories had been spreading for years. The taxation and outright stealing were something nearly every farmer experienced. A few chickens were swiped from the Tilridge farm by loyalists who wished to support the army ravaging the cities of Trenton and Philadelphia.

"No good chicken thieves," yelled Tilly after the chicken's disappearance was discovered. In her own language, she cursed on them.

"Hush, Tilly!" Sarah warned. "We want no trouble." Sarah requested a constable's presence on the first day of the week in order to protect the farm and its meager livestock. "We are only two women with wee ones," she told the local magistrate. "Can you not protect us?" The magistrate reluctantly registered the stolen chickens. He noted that since the two women kept to themselves and had no church affiliation they were ever under the watchful eyes of the British loyalists. People didn't trust quiet hardworking folk. He would see to it that the women were protected by a weekly visit.

1777

August was an exceptionally hot and dry month. Jeremy Jr. now age fourteen, and his mother made the annual pilgrimage to the tree where his father was buried.

As they approached, they spied a group of horses heading back toward the log church. Another group of horses came down the same road they previously occupied. The two groups met at the tree. Both groups of men in military attire dismounted, their sergeant-at-arms also dismounted. One of the men, a man doing justice to his fourth decade, bowed to a younger man, barely out of his teens.

Jeremy Jr., hungry to fight in the war of the colonies was ecstatic. "Oh ma, look, it's our army," he cried.

Sarah was more reserved. "Get yourself to be quiet now," she told Jeremy Jr. "We'll wait to get to the tree." They stood back and to the side of the church. But close enough to be seen. Sarah overheard a snippet of the conversation.

"Had to meet you, *mon ami*," the younger man said breathlessly. "I travelled a long way from Philadelphia. I know that you do not want me in this battle, *mais pourquoi*? I am so ready to help *votre cause de la liberté*." His enthusiastic smile betrayed his excitement.

"Steady, Lafayette, steady," the elder man said. "I have found little satisfaction in war. But as long as there is evil in men's hearts there will be war."

"*Mais oui*," said Lafayette. "But my dear General Washington..."

The elder man held up his hand to halt Lafayette from speaking, he turned towards Sarah and Jeremy Jr. "May I help you?" he asked with a raised his voice.

They came closer, Sarah curtsied. "Apologies sirs, my name is Sarah Tilridge. My husband is buried under that tree where you stand, almost 14 years to the day. This is his son, Jeremy Jr."

The younger man bowed said, "*Bon jour madame. Je suis Marquis de Lafayette*." The elder man replied, "General George Washington, at your service."

The enclave surrounding the two men stepped aside. The elder man waved Sarah forward. Without waiting for a response, Jeremy Jr. stepped forward and in a tumble of words, relayed the story of his father and the wounded Captain Harold Jensen. How the Captain, suffering from fever from a sustained wound, shot his father and then how his mother tended the wounded Captain. Jeremy Jr. stopped short, "Did you say General Washington?" Jeremy Jr. asked, "Where you Colonel Washington who did right by my mom?' Jeremy questioned.

"Hush," Sarah said softly to Jeremy Jr. Sarah faced General Washington and started to apologize when General Washington interrupted by saying, " What a pleasure to finally meet you Mrs. Tilridge. Your unselfish service to the militia was greatly appreciated."

"*Ah oui,* he is a good son," appraised Lafayette. "You tended a wounded man after he shot your husband, mon Diue! You deserve something more." He turned to Washington. "*Qu'y a-t-il à faire?*"

"There is still more we can do, Lafayette.

"Mrs. Tilridge for your unselfish spirit and continued struggles as a widow raising a family, you should apply for a war widow's stipend."

"*Ah oui,*" said Lafayette as he gave her some coins. "You're a courageous woman."

"And Mrs. Tilridge, should anyone ask, you may use my name, General George Washington."

"Thanks be to both of ye." Sarah looked at the coins. It was more than she had seen in anyone's palm. Jeremy Jr's eyes bulged at the coinage.

General Washington's Captain said, "I'm sorry General, I still don't understand why I'm not to repeat what I just saw and heard to anyone."

David Schneck

"For the last time, General Washington is headed west, we're unable to disclose his exact destination. His meeting today was to dissuade the Marquis de Lafayette from fighting anywhere in the colonies. The marquis is hardly versed in warfare," said the Major.

"Was he not from a military family?" asked the Captain.

"Has nothing to do with it. He's probably the wealthiest man in France and could purchase an entire army."

"That's impressive."

"Well, I will tell you, just because you purchase a horse doesn't mean you should ride it in the Kiplingcotes Derby."

The colonies, bloodied and dazed became an independent nation, while the Tilridge boys grew up and apart. Never seeing eye-to-eye, Adam's impulsiveness got him into scrapes with boys who gathered for an education by an itinerant school master. Jeremy Jr. diligently worked at his books and the farm. He did his best to repair the Tilridge reputation.

As they grew older, Jeremy Jr. learned the less he said to his twin the better. His last fight with his brother, Adam and Jeremy Jr. had was over a young woman whose heart was broken by Adam's cruel pranks. Jeremy warned Adam he'd garner no good fortune, unless he swallowed his pride, apologize to the lady and seek the gentler way.

"Oh, you're a sissified dog!" Adam yelled. "You've been supping at the Quaker Meeting house?" he laughed in his brother's face. "You haven't the courage of an un-weaned pup! Rachel's a gossip and she, by rights, deserved a takedown."

Jeremy's punch knocked Adam to his knees. "Get out!"

Adam was not one to apologize, to anyone. He packed up his bag and without a word of goodbye to his mother or Tilly, left for the land across the Delaware River.

In Pennsylvania, whiskey was a popular and profitable drink, as well as a crucial commodity in the economy of the new states, Adam perfected his skill at the making of liquor. He deftly distilled spirits with a combination of mash and molasses.

The smoky burning flavor was appreciated by all who imbibed. The name of the masterpiece of liquor was actually inspired by a lovely young Quaker woman who told him that it was from the devil, "a sin" she claimed. And though he tried mightily to woo her, she refused and married a like-minded Quaker, pale as a dead fish. But in her honor he named his drink, Adam's Sin.

In Westmorland County, Adam Tilridge was a wealthy man, a dandy prat to the locals. While he dutifully visited home once a year, it brought him nothing but sorrow. Regardless of his generous gifts and monies and even livestock, his mother and Aunt Tilly disapproved of his career. His brother Jeremy Jr. was always absent. Their last argument nearly came to broken bones. Perhaps it was for the best they never set eyes on each other.

The battle of the colonies had ended. But from the noises Adam had been hearing, the new independent nation was swimming in debt. And he knew it was a debt that would be alleviated by someone giving up something. Adam knew that one man's squabbles was another man's bill. When the whiskey barons erupted in open revolt, citizens who were friends now had to choose sides.

"Look at us," Adam raged. "We fought the British and kicked the Redbacks off our soil only to fight amongst ourselves?"

"Tilridge," sighed one exasperated citizen. "You're one of the reasons we're in this predicament. Can you not stand down sir?"

"I?" Adam laughed "It was not I who initiated the tax!"

"Aye, we are targeted," one agreed. "Only those who make 100 barrels or more can afford to toss the collector extra coins."

"Why can't we just pay the taxes and be done with it?"

"Maybe you, but I'll not be taxed into nothing. I despise that simpering Collector Johnson; his smugness is an affront!"

"What's next," roared one farmer. "Will they tax my corn kernels?"

There was a general commotion as two sides tried mightily to voice their opinions simultaneously.

"I agree with Tilridge," an elder said. "While I abhor violence, I don't understand the penalty of a tax on a product like whiskey. It an essential commerce bolstering the foundation of our livelihoods."

"Now, let us cool our heads." One man rose. "I've received notice that the president himself is coming and there's to be a meeting at the Neville's Farm."

"Well now there, Adam, what say you? Our very own president is coming to speak with us."

"Oh aye, and he'll get an earful from me!"

"Please, please," begged Farmer Silas Bowers trying to restore calm. "We must wait to see the fuller picture. We are contributing members of this society. We are farm folk, businessmen, merchants and now citizens of a country that we must tend to."

"By contributing, does that entail allowing the magistrate to confiscate our earnings?" another man scoffed. "Sit back and wait? Are you mad, sir?"

"I'll wager Washington will personally lead militia to our doors!" One of the men stood up who, clearly imbibing his own product, yelled, "I vow, I'll go to Neville's Farm and see to him myself!"

Adam led the charge. The men who followed him were drunk and nearly broke. They descended upon John Neville's farm and proceeded to set it on fire. Neville was armed and shot several times into the darkness. One musket ball found Adam and ripped through his heart. He died quickly.

By the time President Washington arrived, the farm had burned to the ground and the women were tending to the wounded and dead.

President Washington, bowed his head. It made him sick to smell death again, will it ever be out of my nostrils? He listened to the reports and gave his consent to release the bodies to their loved ones. Packed on melting ice in the hot July sun, Adam was returned with honor to his home. No one was the wiser, but rumors arrived ahead of his body. Although a letter of pardon and request for burial was submitted to the Pastor, some were outraged that a murdering drunkard would be permitted to be buried in a church cemetery next his father.

Sarah, Tilly and Jeremy Jr. wanted a quiet burial for Adam, but the town's inhabitants collapsed upon them. Jostled and spit on, Jeremy Jr. reached for his mother and Aunt Tilly, he linked his arms onto each woman's waist and didn't let go.

"Who is that woman?" The magistrate's wife jerked her head at Tilly. "So! Your son was a no-good slaver!"

The mob grew in number and anger. Jeremy Jr. crushed the women closer to him. He was afraid that he was hurting them. "Enough!" he cried. "She is none of your concern. This is my mother and auntie. Disperse!" The new magistrate, called over by his sanctimonious wife, had more British smugness than colonial sensibilities, sought to prove himself. Ah, a crisis to demonstrate my wisdom and elevate my stature, he thought. He waded into the crowd and pretended to listen to the widow and her son's remarks. He nodded sagely. But took note of which way the wind was blowing. The crowd led by one Hannah Somerset insisted that while the widow could bury her son, she would have to answer for the question of slavery. The magistrate knew nothing of the Tilridges or their companion Tilly.

He didn't know of the laws of free men and women. He ordered Tilly be removed from the custody of the Tilridges and returned to the place of her purchase. At Redding's Ferry, Tilly was sold to a slaver headed for islands where they had been short of laborers for the sugar cane and salt harvesting.

They released Sarah and Jeremy Jr. Banished to their farm for their slaving ways. They were to never set foot in Basking Ridge again.

Sarah wept for hours afterward. "She was my friend, my only friend and she was never my slave."

CHAPTER FIVE

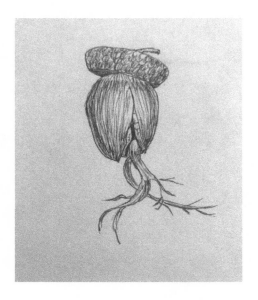

"How pleasing to stand near a rare or new tree! Few are so handsome as this…"
--Henry David Thoreau and the Language of Trees, Richard Higgins, 2017

Driving to his mother's house. He had to tell her the news, had to let her know that the tree on the postcard was going to be gone.

His mother was a bit taken aback and sighed "Isn't there any way to spare it, save it?"

Dan went into explanation overdrive. He'd practiced the speech, prepared himself for the onslaught of questions and had tissues ready for maybe tears. His mother was a very pragmatic woman. If the tree was going to fall on a little kid's head, well she'd be the person out in front carrying a chainsaw. Ken and Gilly were already planning the logistics of how to take the Great Oak Tree down. Still, there was something unsettling about that stupid postcard. Adam told him that Gram Lillian was questioning all living relatives about great grandma's travels during the war and that she went to the Schuylkill County Courthouse to research deeds and marriages.

"Now Mom, listen, I told Ken and Gilly it's going to be a PR nightmare and logistically it's really a tough job. But the tree has to come down and yes, I'll be a part of the team."

"Could there be something in the tree?"

"In a tree? Like what?"

"I don't know, a dead body?"

"What!" Dan exploded. "No that's impossible, Mom what are you saying?"

"Okay, okay I know that's bizarre," admitted Lillian. "But I know we have a connection Dan. I just feel it in my bones."

"Tell you what, Mom, we'll get you to that tree and you'll see," Dan said. "They're doing surveys and maybe an ultrasound I think too."

"Oh, my goodness, like they do for a baby?"

"Sure, it's going to give Ken and Gilly an idea of the kind of decay they're dealing with," Dan explained. "The tree is compromised and it's going to be a delicate process to take it down."

"Why? Can't they just saw it at the bottom?"

Dan laughed. "Uh no, you can't even do that with young healthy trees." He explained that according to Ken and Gilly, there was significant decay reported back in the 1900's. "The church had records that a tree crew had to repair damage to the tree."

Lillian's eyes grew wide. "So, maybe they'll find something inside."

Dan sighed. "Sure, Mom, sure. Like a buried treasure."

"Won't you be embarrassed if there's something inside that tree?"

"Mom, the only thing inside that tree is 7,000 pounds of cement."

"With a dead body inside!" "Like maybe Jimmy Hoffa?"

"I doubt it, mom."

1790

When she first arrived on the island, the turquoise blue waters mesmerized Tilly. She couldn't stop staring. White foam-edged turquois waves lapped the brilliant white sand. The slave ship that she was tossed on ran aground off the coast of Cotton Cay. Though it missed its destination of Cockburn Town, most of the slaves were herded onto row boats and delivered to their new owners. On her rowboat, two slaves strangled the rower, heaved him overboard and set out for the nearest spit of land. Only a few miles south, the shallow waters of Salt Cay with its gentle tides and smell of warming salt drew the slaves, who rowed with all their might.

Tilly squinted at the horizon. There was nothing but sunshine and soft breezes, day after day. She couldn't shake off her restlessness. Tilly searched the horizon for a rescue ship. On this island everything felt upside down. Here, what they called a rake, was no rake. It was a long pole with a flat rudder on its end. And a horse was a tiny mule that never grew over ten hands high. Only a few were tamed and used for work. The enormous bearded frogs that sunned themselves on small rocks, swam like fish and kept their tails. *Not like my home,* she sighed. *My real home with Sarah. Does she miss me? Does Jeremy Jr. even remember me?*

Two years after her arrival on Salt Cay, Tilly's first hurricane increased her desire for home exponentially. With every wave that crashed on the shore, she promised, *I will return home, I will return home.*

She missed the long-frozen winters, giving way to bright springs, seeping into oozing hot summers and gloriously crisp falls. *I will return home; I will return home.* The relentless wind blew until the palm trees bowed down to the sand begging for mercy. Rain slashed at the small huts. The salt pans were overflowing. Two days after the mighty storm, distraught islanders stood knee deep in water. They were trying to push out the excess water to aide in the evaporation process, leaving behind precious salt. The gold of the Caribbean.

Watching the laborious process and its inefficiency, Tilly pulled aside one of the pond's *sallio princeps*. "In my home, we dammed a stream to catch fish, kept them from swimmin' away," she told him. "Here, you need dam the water to keep the salt from swimmin' away."

He shook his head, not understanding. Paul was a smart man, but his despair outweighed his reason. He brushed off the tall woman, who insisted that he fix what was leaking. Tilly liked Paul. He was a tall thin man with a twinkle in his eye. He told Tilly that he served in the navy and loved the sea. He said that all ailments are cured by soaking in the sea. The people on the island used funny terms for things. In their native language "to rest it" meant "to sit it down" and counting was one, two, shree not one, two, three" and these sayings and words made Tilly silently smile.

"Do I not speak good English?" Tilly asked. "Here," she said. "Watch me." She began to pick up and stack rocks and shells to form a dam on the eastern side of one of the salt pans.

Paul halted her progress. "No, no, weez want the salt water."

A frustrated Tilly yelled, "Not in this direction!" Even to her untrained eye, she could walk to the tallest point and see the island's southern-most tip speared the Atlantic, leaving its broad eastern beaches to face little protection against any gale.

She showed him with mime gestures and her slowest and best English, how the storm had raged. It came from the east blowing water and flooding the low-lying ponds, ruining their salt capture. If walls could be built along the eastern side, ponds would be protected from complete devastation. She splashed in the pond, dancing about to demonstrate how the flooding waters could be pushed to the western edges. There, they'd be directed off into established slurries. Deeper ponds could retain the seawater. Though mixed with sand, some of the escaped salt could be rescued after rocks were removed and the water drained.

Paul frowned. Tilly worked for several minutes stacking rocks and shells on the eastern side of the salt pans until other salt hauler and salt pan workers gathered close to observe. Word spread of her walls and her ideas. Tilly was brought to meet with the engineers of the salt pans. Desperate to avoid another disaster, they accepted Tilly's help to design a natural barrier, similar to the smaller wall she already erected. With Tilly hovering over their shoulders, the engineers devised a more complicated series of smaller salt pans where windmills could move water within the change of the tides, intricate canals and sluices to induce flooding waters to exit the salt pans. The windmills were constructed to utilize the Cay's breezes to move the sea water and salt brine from larger ponds to smaller salt pans. Tilly also suggested that the canvas on the windmills should be removed prior to any hurricane since tall structures were no match for gale force winds.

As far back as any living islander could remember, it was the only time a woman was sought for advice pertaining to matters of civil engineering. And when the next hurricane hit the island, the Salt Pans and windmills survived but sadly two babies lost their lives.

Their mothers mourned for a month and the entire island mourned with them. Thousands of miles away in their comfortable homes, the salt merchants had little concept of the misery hurricanes inflicted upon the salt workers.

The Cay had no outright established government. Without protection, it was at the mercy of pirates and worse, salt trade ships. Pirates picked up a few lone islanders for slaves and the salt trader raided the island of as much of the salt as they could without recompense. Thus islanders were forced to protect their only form of currency, "White Gold". Female inhabitants held small knife-like weapons carved from broken conch shells. They tucked one or two on their person, in their corsets or under their skirts. The male inhabitants made much larger hand-held weapons they openly carried on their belts. They posted a lookout on the bluff to watch for pirates and unwanted trade ships and should any unwanted pirates or sailors arrive, they were greeted at the dock with men waving shell machetes. In time Britain claimed the island and regularly sent ships to pick up salt. On one of the trips for salt, a British sailor, taking a moment to stretch his legs, took a shine to Tilly. He followed her out of the salt pan and to the nearby holding areas. Tilly, in an attempt to avoid him, dropped her rake and pushed her half-filled salt cart into the shed near the dock. "Hey lass," he rasped. "Mind if I have a turn?"

She whirled around. Before she could cry out, the sailor cupped his hand over her mouth pinned her against one of the huge salt mounds and bit her neck. Unable to reach for her conch-knife, she responded by smearing a handful of sun-scalded salt into his eyes.

He roared in pain, and reeled back, releasing her. Tilly ran to the tiny commons at the point of Deane's Dock. She confronted a British Royal Naval officer who barely listened to her pleas for help. He told her to, "Remove yourself from my presence." He tried to walk away but an indignant Tilly blocked his path. The officer ordered his men to return to the ship. He grabbed Tilly by her head covering, dragged her into the merchant's abandoned office and assaulted her.

Paul did his best to intervene. He pounded on the door and smashed the window pane, he heard Tilly screaming and fighting back. He cheered her efforts, when he heard the officer's shrieks of pain. Paul was pulled away from the door and beaten back by sailors who returned having heard the commotion. Islanders surrounded the sailors. As the officer emerged holding a bloodied cheek, he took in the situation. His Majesty's Navy Officer and sailors never retreated so fast to the safety of their ship.

"Never come back, all a ya!" yelled Paul. He and the islanders threw everything they could at the running sailors— stones, shells, rakes. They climbed aboard their ships with pieces of the island stuck in their skin.

Tilly was cared for by the women for two days. She didn't return to the salt pans until a week later. It took longer for her spirit to mend. She was sullen and silent. The islanders showed nothing but a gentle sweetness. Small flowers were tucked by her pallet at night. A small crock of aloe for her sore parts. And extra gull egg for lunch. At first, Tilly felt as though they pitied her, treated her like a hurt animal. When she finally did speak to the islanders, they told her it was by no means the first time a woman or a man was brutalized in such a way. They admired her strength and her courage to fight back.

When Paul came to visit. He shook his head. "So bad, so sorry."

Tilly sobbed. "This is a horrible place. Why do you not leave?"

"We are Belongers," he said. "We belong to the island and it belongs to us. It takes care of us sometime an' we take of dis an' das. Best weez can."

Much to her horror, Tilly began to grow a belly. Without symptoms of sickness or hunger—everyone was always hungry--her pregnancy was a secret. When her belly became obvious, the Cay's "Bush Medicine Healer" suggested a tincture of rosary tea, salt water, and aloe. "To rid you of the *bâtarde*."

Tilly couldn't bring herself to drink it. Despite the child's monstrous beginnings, it was now the only living thing she was close to, her only living relative, her nearest kin.

Tilly's engineering innovations extended to harvesting rain water. Without any springs or naturally occurring fresh water, islanders used cisterns and barrels to collect rain water. Unfortunately, rain barrels were no match for the forceful trade winds that blew. With her experience as a farmer, she was able to stabilize a barrel to capture the rain without tipping over and spilling its precious commodity by filling a fifth of the barrel with scoured salt-free shells and sand-filled linen bags, the weighted barrels rarely toppled. She then recommended that barrel be constructed with holes so that the water would flow into larger underground holding tanks. A small communal tank-cart was outfitted with wheels to bring water to the salt fields to help hydrate salt harvesters. It was better for uninterrupted work. It took time for workers to go in search of fresh water.

Control of the Cay passed into the hands of the Bahamians. Though still technically British, they were influenced by more compassionate abolition-minded Americans. The salt import company in Philadelphia paid the Belonger's well. Setting up a small trading center at Deane's Dock, Salt Cay's primary export became the primary import of Brown & Harriet of Philadelphia.

Tilly's innovations along with more productive salt workers delighted the salt barons. Little Salt Cay harvested more salt than all the other islands combined. "As long as there is salt water, there will be salt," Tilly told them.

In a gesture of magnanimity, the proprietors of Brown & Harriet bestowed upon Tilly a writ to proclaim her a freed woman. Tilly took the news graciously, but explained that she was already a freed woman and had been abducted and sold to a slaver. This injustice was never addressed. As such, she only desired to buy a passage home to New Jersey. She wanted to be reunited with her family back on the Tilridge farm and introduce her son Oliver to them.

Each month, as Tilly waited for the funds to buy passage to the now United States, there were inevitable excuses. She hadn't understood their reluctance to take a mother and a newborn baby, still she waited for approval.

Brown & Harriet, unwilling to let this creative and productive woman go, dangled other carrots in front of Tilly's nose. *Why not a formal education?* The Sisters of Charity of the Blessed Virgin Mary were excellent teachers having established excellent primary schools in Philadelphia. One or two could be dispatched to teach, not only Tilly, but all the Cay residents. *Why not a home of your own?* A house for Tilly, constructed just so, to be the envy of all the others. *Perhaps a horse and cart?* Tilly's own personal transportation.

She rejected all their bribes. "I don't need an education. And I already have a home." She shook her head. "What are you thinking? What would I do with a horse and cart on an island that I can walk around in one day?" The Brown & Harriet communications office cringed. How to inform the proprietors that their beneficence had been rejected by a former slave with more common sense than their Board members?

Tilly stewed for days. "How stupid do they think I am, Paul?"

"They trying to catch fish with a palm leaf," he laughed. "Day don't know you."

Each month Tilly was more and more anxious to return home. Her memory was leaving her mind. In the middle of the night the baby cried for her. As she nursed the little boy, she dug deep and couldn't remember Sarah's face. She remembered her last day under a large tree, clinging to Jeremy Jr. for safety. She wept. *How could I forget my Sarah?* The last time Tilly asked for return passage to her home, she was told that it could not be so because the entire country—was in an enormous schism. It wasn't safe to enter the country unless one had papers. Tilly produced the declaration of her freedom. It was rejected. "You need the seal of the colonial governor," she was told by the dock man. "Unless you have a great deal of money or a boat, there's not a port that will allow you entrance." The rejection of her pleas to return home gathered in her heart like an enormous iron anchor. It thudded with an awful pain.

One year then another passed and soon Oliver was a boy needing a father. Tilly and Paul grew closer to each other. They worked together in the Salt Pans and in the evening after dinner, they enjoyed listening and playing music. Paul was a wonderful musician and played well. In time the two fell into a rhythm and soon fell in love. And although Tilly missed New Jersey, she couldn't leave Paul. He had become her rock on the Little Rock Island. They married and had three children making them a family of six with Tilly's son Oliver. The first of their children was a boy with eyes that shone brighter than his father's eyes and they named him Eros. After Eros, Tilly gave birth to twin girls. The first of the twins to be born was named Sandra and the second one was named Sonia. Eros grew up to be a very handsome and charismatic man which helped him to be very successful in a number of retail businesses on the island. Sandra grew up to be the "Bell of the Ball". She was tall, thin and curvy with olive skin and long black hair. But she was as rebellious as her a mother in not being controlled by a man. Sandra wanted a boat of her own to enter the trade world and sail away on the wind which she eventually did. As for Sonia, she was as beautiful as her sister and more reserved like her father. She was content to stay with her mother and father and build a future on Salt Cay. She built a rental cottage on the South end of the island and named it "Sonia's Hideaway". She also became interested in island politics and was successful in becoming the first woman to hold a government position on the island. Tilly's first son Oliver was also handsome and strong. His skin was fair and his hair was light brown and his last name was different from his brother and sisters. When he became of age, Tilly told him the little that she know about his father and lied about why she gave Oliver her last name and not his father's but avoided telling him how he raped her. Later as a young adult, he wanted to know his real father. So he got a job on a ship that was headed to England. After a few years of searching he learned that his father was thrown overboard during a violent storm off the coast of Virginia. His body was never found. Oliver returned to Salt Cay and related what he learned about his father to Tilly. Tilly was not unhappy to hear about the Officer's death but she hid her feelings from Oliver.

Oliver settled back into life on Salt Cay - fishing and working for the salt barons. He was enjoying the hard simple life of the cay until one day when a Merchant ship docked at the White House and a beautiful tall red haired woman stepped on hard ground for the first time in a year. She was breathtaking, Oliver looked like a stunned mullet standing there with his mouth gaping. She introduced herself as Kayleigh O'Reily from the Emerald Isle of Ireland. "Do you have a name, looking at Oliver?" she inquired. "Ol- Ol- Oliver, Oliver Tilridge," he finally managed to mutter. It was love at first sight for both of them and it wasn't long before they were married. Oliver and Kayleigh were very adventurous and they loved the ocean. Using a small portion of Kayleigh's inheritance, they purchased a sloop and sailed to all of the surrounding islands. They made a decent living by buying, selling and trading needed commodities as they traveled from island to island. They made enough money to purchase two tickets for a voyage from the Bahamas to Ireland. Kayleigh couldn't wait to see her family again. During the voyage

Kayleigh gave birth to a baby boy. They named him Tristan. The O'Reily family was thrilled to see a young Irish Blok and they convinced Oliver and Kayleigh to remain in Ireland until their little lad was five years old. During the ages of 4 and 5, Tristan heard the stories and legends of the Irish people and how a tree could speak through an instrument made from its wood. Tristan, like his parents, loved the ocean – even the cold waters of Ireland. Tristan's parents became restless and felt a great urge to return to Salt Cay.

Tilly and Paul heard via the island grape vine that Oliver and his family were returning home. Tilly and Paul, Eros and his family and Sonia were waiting at Deane's dock when Oliver and his family arrived. Tilly took to young Tristan like a sponge to water.

Tilly was now up in years and she spent most of her time with Tristin and her other grandchildren. She told them all about New Jersey and her life on the Tilridge Farm. They learned about the beautiful trees that turned a vibrant color in the fall each year. She told them about the Great Oak Tree and the legends of its song and spirit. She explained how her namesakes (Jeremy and Sarah Tilridge and their sons Adam and Jeremy Jr. and his family) were buried under the Great Oak Tree.

Tristan and Tilly had a special bond between them. Both of them talked and dreamed about going to America and back to New Jersey to see the Tilridge Farm and the Great Oak Tree. Tilly gave Tristan her favorite Queen Conch Shell with the hope of him taking it back to Basking Ridge, New Jersey.

One night Tilly dreamed of the Great Oak Tree and standing under it with Jeremy Jr. They were clinging to each other as they did back in 1777 and this time he didn't let go of her. Tilly viewed the dream as an omen of her passing and joining the Spirit of the Great Oak Tree and her loved ones. Within two days of her dream, Tilly passed away quietly in her sleep. Tilly was 102 years old at the time of her passing which was a testament to having a long life on the quiet island of Salt Cay. Tilly's spirit would live on in her four children, her seven grandchildren and future generations.

Tristan was consumed by grief and he vowed that he would travel to America and find the Tilridge Farm. He would take his grandmother's Queen Conch Shell and bury it on Sarah Tilridge's grave under the Great Oak Tree.

CHAPTER SIX

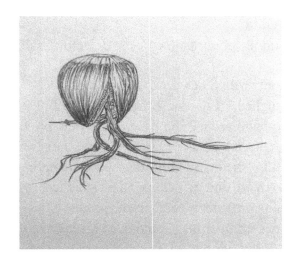

"I think that I shall never see
A poem as lovely as a tree…"

--*Joyce Kilmer, 1913*

He drove his mother to see the oak.

The ride was quiet. Every so often punctuated by a question from his mother. *Who's going to be there? How long will it take? What happens after the ultrasound?*

"And no," Dan said. "There's no way to save it, Mom."

Ken and Gilly were already there, setting up the unit and planning how to get the best visuals.

Pastor Tom had the local police block off the main street that morning to reduce the noise. Ken needed to have as little motion and noise as possible. Both would interfere with his measurements.

"Oh, look at that," Lillian said as she patted the surface like a small child.

"This here is an ultrasonic decay detector," said Ken. "We call it udder."

Lillian only rolled her eyes.

Gilly laughed. "She doesn't get it, okay?" He wrapped a black Velcro band around the base of the massive trunk. Every two feet he placed small white units no larger than phone chargers. Gilly then gathered the wires dangling from the bottom to a main unit which he also attached to the Velcro band. He set a computer screen on the ground.

Lillian peered over his shoulder. "This is so exciting."

Although the church lot and the cemetery were cordoned off with caution tape, a crowd gathered to watch.

Dan knew there would always be some sort of logistical, not to mention a PR nightmare attached to the take down of this oak. Okay by him. People were curious. But as part of the team, he promised he'd help maintain some semblance of order. "Hey folks," he said to the gathering of 20 or so, "let's move back a little."

The crowd acquiesced and moved back to a safer space, but held their cell phones higher.

"Just what are you guys doing?" one person asked.

"Taking an ultrasound of the tree," Dan said.

"What!" The crowd was surprised. "Seriously, like a baby?"

Dan laughed. "It's a specialized machine that checks for deep decay."

Gilly, overheard Dan's discussion. He turned on the screen and yelled, "It's a girl!"

There was a chuckle from the crowd. Dan explained to them, that while it was highly unlikely that the tree was pregnant, significant decay had been reported as early as the 1900's. "Back then, they used tar and cement to repair it and seal off any decay."

Lillian came over to Dan and whispered, "Won't you be embarrassed if there's something inside that tree."

Dan shook his head. "No dead bodies, Mom, he whispered back." He and his mother walked back to Ken and Gilly. Both men were staring at the computer screen and frowning.

"What the hell is that?" Gilly asked.

1863

Tristan Tilridge was happy to be going anywhere that wasn't Salt Cay. Unlike most islanders he didn't belong. He pointed out time and time again that he didn't come from the island. He was born on the ocean and that he was committed to returning home to his grandmother's farm in New Jersey in America.

His mother Kayleigh, as happy as she could be that her son was going to spread his wings, was broken hearted. She told him that she knew there was a wild adventurous streak in him that he inherited from her and his father Oliver. "I see the way you work in the salt pan, my love," she said. "I also see how your heart soars on gulls' wings longing to be somewhere else."

Tristan couldn't argue, his heart was longing to be at the horizon. He remembered being in Ireland when he was young, he sailed around Salt Cay in a sloop by the time he was twelve and now he was sailing to the other islands around Salt Cay. He wanted to be in America.

"I hoped you could be staying," she sniffled. "But if you stayed my love, you would be so, so sad."

Again, he could not argue. His happiest day was waving goodbye with his grandmother's Queen Conch Shell in hand.

He landed in Virginia at the worst time in the state's history. Virginia was on the verge of seceding from the rest of the nation. As a darker than puritan white man, he never gave or explained his true background to others. How do you explain his mixed culture and race of British white, African black and Irish white?

Dashing and handsome, his shy manner added to his charm. He went from the docks to the next boat that sailed up the Jamestown River. Landing in Richmond, he applied to the new consulate and was hired as personal assistant to the ambassador to The Bahama Islands, in the West Indies.

While Tristan enjoyed entrance into some of the highest echelons of Southern society, he observed with chagrin, life was more equitable on his poor little Salt Cay. He couldn't stomach the cruel treatment of the people who looked so much like his island family.

The decision to leave Virginia after only a year's stay was easy. He vaguely apologized for leaving his position, and never looked back. He crossed the Mason Dixon line and joined the Federals. Enlisting in the Union Army was not so easy. He was rejected by the Calvary because he was unable to stay on top of a moving a horse. The island donkeys weren't exactly comparable to charging a bay mare in field drills.

Finally, Tristan was accepted into the infantry. Clumsy with a rifle, he prayed he'd never be challenged. He was able to drill without resting for hours, which pleased the officers.

General Burnside ordered Tristan's regiment into battle to engage the enemy in Virginia. As they marched south, Tristan heard the men sing:

I'm goin' down south to beat them Johnny rebs.
Coming home victorious and sweet Sally I will wed.
Gonna wrap my arms around her
and Old Glory, my precious flag concur.

Tristan knew they sang to keep their spirits high. Deep down all of them had had enough of the gallantry of the war. He had given up on believing he was fighting for the cause. *What was "the cause?"* He couldn't discern who was right, because in the middle of the battle, all he was trying to do was to kill somebody before they killed him. It was a daily battle to survive. The heat, the insects, the disease and the despair.

While the war raged on, he made good friends and watched them die, he seen so many awful things, but the worst of it, was the smell. The rotting flesh, the smell of men's spilt innards. The aftermath of the battles all smelled the same, like one large bloody latrine. When it rained, heavy down pours took away the smell if only for a brief moment but only to replace by a fetid stench of open sewer and bloody sweat.

In his last confrontation, Tristan heard that to save men, the army engineers proposed a plan. To cause a major disruption, miners were to dig a tunnel under the railroad track that ran from Richmond to Petersburg, thus depriving the enemy of supplies. And forcing them to retreat.

Once the miners began, they couldn't be stopped. "They dig like hungry little moles," remarked one officer. "They're fast and straight." The army was only too glad to have them. Tristan's platoon was assigned the task of supporting the moles by relocating the newly dug soil from the tunnel. His fellow solider, Chester Highnickle, carried the shovel and Tristan wheeled a small wooden cart to and from the unloading area.

Why am I working like this? He thought. I carted all day on Salt Cay. The only difference here is that instead of white salt, it is brown dirt.

While his job felt long and relentless, the moles dug the tunnels in an efficient process. Three miners dug in single file. The first went in, gouged out a chunk of earth, turned and pushed that chunk to the front of the tunnel. The second followed and did the same, as did the third. The three men repeated these actions for an hour. Then woodsmen went in and shored up the roof and the sides of the tunnel to keep it from collapsing before its time. Tristan's team kept the earth moving and as instructed built a small formicary to protect the rest of the troops to the northwest of the tunnel. The rest of the platoon simply dug trenches.

Lastly, the demolition team entered to affix explosives. The entire tunnel had to collapse in order that the railroad track would sink and splinter, cutting the South's supply lines solidly in half. To Tristan it was a huge waste of manpower and time.

"Look at that," said Chester. He jerked his chin at the oncoming horses. They both marveled as a carriage laden with bottles of clear liquid passed them, gingerly navigating a path to the opening.

"What's is that?" asked Tristan.

"That's the nitro cart," Chester responded. "There's enough in that buggy to blow up half the planet."

Tristan instinctively stepped back.

"Oh, don't you worry," Chester assured him. "They know what they're doing. Still, don't get too close, just in case they overdo it. There's plenty there to destroy the track from here to the Oklahoma Territory."

It was a hot, July morning, the air was heavy and still. Word was that at any moment, General Burnside would give the order to detonate the tunnel.

"We got 'em," cackled Chester. "General Lee is pinned down in Petersburg!"

"Why don't we attack him now?"

"No, you idiot, because we blow up the tunnel, cut them off and then they surrender," he argued. "There can't be more than, I dunno, five or six thousand Johnny Rebs if I heard it right."

A shout was heard and the men were called to order. The instructions were simple, back up, blow up and then charge.

The eardrum-ripping blast knocked every man off his feet. In one moment, a crater the size of Vance Lake was created. Any man or material too close to the epi-center was instantly vaporized. Tristan behind the formicary, crawled over the dirt unable to see or hear. He called out for Chester. He couldn't hear any responses.

The Union soldiers underestimated the power of the explosives, ignored requests and stood too close. They nearly obliterated themselves.

The Confederates, also reeling from the shock of the explosion, quickly recovered and launched several counterattacks. Tristan could see a swarm of gray. He also noted the stars on the shoulders of dreaded Major William "Billy" Mahone. He needed no prodding from anyone as he pried the dead owner's hands off of an Enfield rifle. He shoved a Minie ball down its bore and charged.

It was dubbed the Battle of the Crater. Unit after unit of Union soldiers fell into the crater only to find there was no way out but up into the Confederate rifles. "It was like shooting fish in a barrel," one rebel soldier bragged. Most of Tristan's platoon caught at the bottom of the crater, made no attempt to escape. Confused, deaf and unseeing, they milled about, until one by one they succumbed to any and all manner of artillery aimed at them.

The severe casualties rattled Tristan. He couldn't stop staring at the dead bodies. A ball caught him in the shoulder. He fell backwards. Still hearing the whizzing of Minie balls he crawled over two bodies and laid down. He waited for a pause. Taking a chance, he crawled over three more. He looked across the other side of the crater. There were more bodies lying on the ground than there were standing.

By the time the sounding bugle called "Retreat" there were few ears to hear it. Tristan and a handful of men who had crawled out of the crater, scurried at dusk to the safer northern post. Comparing notes, the men realized even before they were informed, that the Union suffered a devastating loss.

Tristan's wound granted him a stroke of luck by landing him in a small field hospital in Pennsylvania. He was moved there to repair damage to his shoulder that couldn't be addressed anywhere else. His naturally quiet manner was misconstrued as mental fragility. He was released without any urgings to re-enlist and fight for the cause. The surgeon told Tristan's commanding officer, "He survived the Battle of the Crater." Looking at Tristan with pity. "He's not going to be right in the head."

The surgeon was right. For weeks after his discharge, Tristan had nightmares. Dead men were speaking to him, begging for mercy. He never fully regained his hearing. And although his spirit and love of life was dampened, he courted and married a lovely northern lady. He never wanted to fight or talk of war ever.

He settled down as far from the battle as he could—but there wasn't a family in the states that hadn't been scarred by the war. He and his wife Annie Hoy, were blessed with three children. Even through Tristan's mind blocked the war, he remembered the stories and legends of Ireland and Salt Cay and he told them to his children. He told them about their great grandmother Tilly. He told them how he had vowed to return to the Tilridge Farm in New Jersey and bury a Queen Conch Shell on Sarah Tilridge's grave under the Great Oak Tree in Basking Ridge. So before his death, Tristan begged his son Richard to promise to fulfill the vow that he could not carry out.

Richard inherited his father's wanderlust and after his father died, Richard Tilridge travelled to Johnstown, Pennsylvania. It was near the end of the 19th century, humankind was making amazing strides and the whole city hummed with industry. He was able to get a job easily as a clerk in the dispatch office at the newly minted depot of the Pennsylvania Railroad. While the city was technically a transfer point along the Pennsylvania Main Line Canal that paralleled the Conemaugh River, the railroad proved to be the chief mode of transport. And the railroad was in great need of minds and hands to keep it on track. Coal mines and steel plants powered the ever-burgeoning city in monies and in growth. New jobs were popping up like flowers in spring.

Johnstown was in a narrow valley and Richard was certain this valley would be his home, a good place to live. He was lucky to find modest accommodations at a boarding home on Union Street, run by a crabby old Bavarian transplant.

Richard's roommate Robert Slattery distrusted their landlady. "I've heard her husband passed away in the old country," he whispered to Richard late one night. "I'll wager the old crank has him stuffed somewhere in the nether regions of this place."

However suspicious the landlady was, she made sure that breakfast and dinner were served promptly. Rent was collected at the end of the month and all renters were men. No female guests were permitted inside. A rather useless rule, Robert would joke. "Have you even seen a female anywhere near close to the Union Street?" Competition was stiff for female companionship. Most lovely young ladies were able to marry mid-level managers whose families who owned large swaths of land or invested in the businesses. The largely-working class, male population had only work and each other to keep them company.

Richard set aside all thoughts of marrying anyone until one unusually warm April, he walked a different route home. Main Street was a watery mess from spring thaw and he had no choice but to slog up Walnut and cross over on Lincoln.

His heart stopped and his feet froze to the slate walkway. Amidst the flutter and frenzy of furniture, parcels and fixtures being carried into a home, a lovely young woman stood holding the hands of two children. The children jumped up and down as boxes were whisked by them in an efficient emptying of a large moving cart. The woman turned her head and for the barest of moments, their eyes met. Richard nodded a greeting. The woman gave no acknowledgement but turned her attention to the children. An older woman appeared at the steps. She gestured for the children and the younger woman to come inside. They cried, "Mama, mama!" The mother guided the children inside, but gave instructions to the younger woman. The younger woman went to the cart and retrieved a small doll. The younger woman returned to the older woman and handed her the doll. "Yes, thank you, please give it to Betsy and see to the children's baths," said the older woman.

Richard's heart thumped in his chest. She wasn't married, they weren't her children. The following day, he peppered his roommate Robert, the boarding house gossiper with all sorts of questions. "Was she just a nursemaid? A companion?" Robert demurred. "I don't know."

"How would I go about discovering her identity?"

Robert frowned. "Well, you could go back and ask her."

"No! What kind of friend are you? I'd look the fool asking about her origins. I've never been formally introduced. Ask her indeed!"

"It's the fastest way."

"I need a more discreet way, please" he urged his friend. "What about Barrett? Doesn't he work for the Pinkerton Detective Agency?"

"Oh, good god man! What is she, a criminal?"

"All I need is a last name."

"Oh, blast it all, I'll see if he can help," Robert groaned. "Now can we go to bed?"

Richard's unrelenting harassment of Robert did produce answers and two days later seized upon the best bit of information that Barrett the one-time detective-in-training provided. The hearty Germans who never saw an Asian before tittered that she was from the Monongahela tribe. Her name was Sachiko.

"Sachiko," Richard repeated, settling the name on his lips and his heart. "Is that it? No first name?"

"Sorry friend, that's all he has. She's the governess or nanny to a wealthy family." Barrett was able to learn that the father, Seth Rink, worked as an investor in the Johnstown National Bank. He had transferred from Pittsburgh. Mrs. Adele Rink, nee Bolton was equally wealthy.

Sachiko was the loveliest thing he'd ever seen, like an exotic flower. Her glossy black hair framed her pale as fresh milk face. And he would tell her so. In less than a week, he walked to the river at just the right time to intercept her on her return walks by the river.

Before he could help himself, Richard said to her, "You are the finest thing I've ever seen."

The children giggled.

Sachiko nodded politely and said, "Please excuse me." She gathered the children to her like a mother hen and promptly headed home.

Her dismissal didn't dismay him. He walked on air all the way home. In his thoughts, he nicknamed her, Sachi.

On Tuesdays and Thursdays, he followed Sachi home from the river. The little park had a grassy area where Johnstown residents could stroll, enjoying the view.

While he followed her and the children home, he'd speak to her about everything and anything. Did she think it was going to rain? Did she like music? Did she play an instrument? What kind? Was she a Christian? Could she smell the honeysuckle from the hedgerow? What did she think of the river? Didn't the train make a lonely whistle?

One subject garnered an actual response. "Now, take this town," he began. "Do you know it wasn't always called Johnstown?"

One of the children, Betsy answered. "I do, I do," she said jumping up and down. "I know that, they called it, um, it's a funny name that's hard to pronounce."

"Yes," Sachiko spoke for the first time, although to instruct the children or respond to him he wasn't sure. "It was originally called Conemaugh," she supplied. "But no one knew how to pronounce or spell it correctly." She bowed her head. "It is not the first instance where people of this country mispronounce and misspell foreign words."

Richard was in awe. Her voice was soft and clear and had a slight lisp that tugged on his heart. Had an onlooker caught a glimpse of his face, they'd recommend a physician. Unable to breathe or move, he remained frozen to the spot and helplessly watched Sachi and the children walk away. Betsy turned and gave a fluttery wave, and then they were gone.

The day after he drummed up the courage to make a request to her. When Betsy and her brother Eli were focused on catching a toad, Richard approached Sachi. "Do you think we could stroll, just the two of us?"

"Goodness no," Sachi sniffed and tossed up her chin. "You are clerk at a railroad office."

He smiled at her. "Maybe now but it will not always be so."

"Oh?"

"I have ambitions."

Sachi's lips curled up into a smile on her tiny heart-shaped face. "What kind of ambitions?"

"I should like to own the B&O Railroad."

She laughed. The delightful sound bubbled up and floated around him.

"Don't you doubt me," he cautioned her. "It takes time and patience and—"

"Much money," she finished.

"And, yes, that takes patience too."

"There's an old proverb, 'where you put your hands, there is your heart.' It means what you work hardest at, it is there you will find your life."

"I believe I have found my life; it is with you."

Sachi was silent.

After that day, Richard was unrelenting. He worked hard. His life's purpose was to capture Sachi's heart. He set aside money and invested in the railroad.

"Ho, ho," cried Robert after he handed Richard a piece of mail from Harding & Philips. "Another check from your stockbroker?"

"Yes, though it's none of your damn business," Richard responded. "I don't squander my savings."

Robert grew serious. "Well, I never, you really do love her, don't you?"

Richard knew that in order to marry Sachi, he'd have to make a deal with the Rink family. How would they let go of a perfectly wonderful nanny?

He gathered the courage to approach Sachi's employer. Sachi confessed that her true family, the family of her birth, was in Japan. They were poor fishermen and sold her to the wealthy American family—the Rinks. In Japan, the Meiji government invested in railway lines and the Rinks were on a tour of Japan seeking commerce and trade. They took her in as a girl of twelve and gave her family payment. She told Richard, she was fortunate, many less fortunate girls were sold into sex slavery.

The Rinks were all too glad to give their blessing. Richard expected more of a challenge in asking Sachi's employer for her hand. But Mrs. Rink had been speaking to the ladies at the Union Street Garden Club and they insisted she procure a British governess. It was a necessity for her children's upbringing in the nouveau riche society. And it simply wouldn't do to have an oriental girl under the same roof. Mrs. Rink also had the same feeling but her worries were more directed towards Mr. Rink.

The only people who objected to the match were the children. Betsy and Eli were devastated. They begged Sachi and Richard to take them along.

"We'll behave," promised Eli. "We'll never get our feet muddy."

Sachi smiled. "That is nearly impossible in this town. And for someone who loves to chase frogs and toads, can you?"

Eli looked down at his already muddied shoes. He sniffled.

"He's just silly. Oh, please, we'll never be disobedient," Betsy promised, tears in her eyes. "Please don't leave."

Sachi explained gently that she would miss them, but it was important to move to the next level of growing up. "We cannot always be playing with our dolls, now, can we?"

On May 31, Richard Tilridge and Sachiko Tusori were married in the small All Saints Chapel adjacent to the First Presbyterian Church on Lincoln Street. They promised their love would endure forever.

One hour later, the South Fork Dam collapsed, the unstoppable floodwaters hit Johnstown.

CHAPTER SEVEN

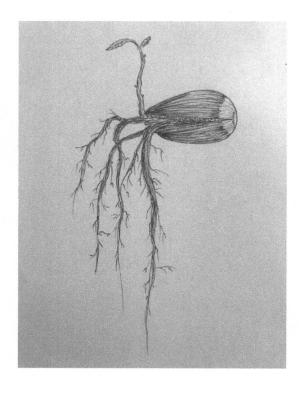

"From a small seed a mighty trunk may grow."
--Aeschylus, 525 BC

Dan, his mother Lillian, Ken and Gilly stared at the screen. Dan repeated Ken's question. "What the hell is that?"

"I don't know," Gilly said. "Maybe it's a nail or something?"

"Hmm, I don't think so, looks too big," said Ken.

"Oh, how big?" asked Lillian. "It looks like a finger to me."

The men looked at her. "Uh, Mom," said Dan. "It's not a finger. It's probably just a big nail or something." Although Dan hated to admit it, the object on the screen did look larger than a common flat-headed siding nail.

"Yeah, Dan's right," Gilly told Lillian. "Organic matter, unless it's some type of decay isn't going to show up like that."

"Gotta be something metal," Ken said. "Hey Dan, you wouldn't happen to have that metal detector handy, would you?"

Dan was surprised that Ken remembered his favorite tool. "Yeah, I was using it the other day."

"Searching for lost treasure?" Lillian teased.

"Uh, no Mom, I was trying to make sure I didn't ruin another saw chain," Dan retorted. "Also, I can't tell you how many ruined blades I have when I mill wood like this."

"What do you mean?"

"When I mill any raw lumber, I'm at the mercy of the wood," he said. "People are careless and leave nails, wire, metal stakes, heck, even horseshoes in a tree. And when I saw through it, it is metal tearing metal."

"Oh dear, not good," Lillian commiserated.

"Nope."

"But still there might be something more to what's inside the tree, that you can sort of see?" Lillian pressed.

"Yeah," Ken agreed. "Can you get that metal detector?"

Dan unloaded his metal detector. And for the eighteenth time that day kicked himself for bringing his mother along. "Okay, so they found a big nail or something," he conceded. "There are plenty of nails in trees."

His mother was so insistent. "But please can you check that branch or higher up there in the trunk?" she begged. She was practically jumping up and down.

Dan had scanned the tree and the nail-shaped object was larger than anyone had guessed. It looked long and flat, almost like a blade. But he didn't tell his mother. He simply put the detector away. Then the conversation got more serious.

"We're not really here looking for metal objects," Gilly admitted. "Sure, you can find things like that. Trees typically grow around wounds made by anything."

"Could the tree grow around other things?"

"Sure, but what we're really looking for is decay," he said.

"What happens now?" Lillian asked.

"We keep looking," Ken said. "We've got to get a handle on how bad the interior is."

"They can keep looking for dead bodies," Lillian whispered. She giggled into her hand.

1889

It was a wet, dark Friday. The dreariness was no match for their spirits, Richard Tilridge and Sachiko Tusori were married in the small All Saints Chapel adjacent to the Frist Presbyterian Church on Lincoln Street. The only witnesses to the wedding were Robert Slattery, Nathan Bedrich (a colleague and boardinghouse mate) and the Rink Family. Betsy and Eli were permitted to attend.

Sachi had admitted that the thunder, lightning and rain prior to her wedding day was not a sign of good fortune. She did understand that not everyone shared her concern. The Rink's Italian housemaid informed them that rain on a wedding day meant showers of good luck.

Richard did his best to allay Sachi's fears but he too had a heavy feeling about the unrelenting rain. He also couldn't change his work schedule. At the office, leaves were chosen via lottery. He won the short leave of two days, off Friday returning Monday. Longer leaves were "under discussion" at headquarters in Baltimore. Robert had told him that the management down there was granted an unheard-of annual leave that consisted of five days--Monday through Friday.

"That's never going to happen here," Robert scoffed. He stared up at the sky. More rain. Water had been oozing through streets since the day before.

Richard's choice of days was limited by the pastor at All Saints. The very reverend Percy Hadivahl, insisted he perform the ceremony on his least busy day. "Wednesdays, I meet with the Ladies of the Temperance Society and the elders meet with me on Thursdays. Saturdays, I prepare my sermons and attend to parish business." And Sundays, Reverend Hadivahl told Richard, were of course his busiest days. Richard understood why Reverend Hadivahl kept Mondays and Tuesdays for himself. "Pfft, that fisher of men is a dabbler," dismissed Robert when Richard informed his best man of the date and time. "Hadivahl enjoys a fishing trip or two at Conemaugh Lake."

The exclusive South Fork Sportsmen's Club had some tempting bass as well as lunkers imported for serious fishermen, Robert told Richard. "And I'm not saying he's poaching fish, but I don't think he's a guest." The Reverend sent a note to Richard the week prior to express his apologies but he requested that Richard and his bride-to-be, as well as all witnesses were to arrive at the sanctuary after noon, midday, since the Garden of Gethsemane Fellows met on Friday mornings when his wedding should have been held.

Truth be told, the Reverend had another, less godly, reason for moving Richard's wedding into the afternoon. Passersby were lighter in the afternoon; less carriages, fewer workers. He didn't want to be seen officiating the rather unorthodox ceremony. He wouldn't have done it if it weren't for the prodding's (and generous donations) of Mrs. Rink. She had advised him that while the laws in Pennsylvania prohibited marrying out of one's race, she needed his help. Mr. Rink was caught looking at the children's nanny with a less-than-fatherly eye. And it was either, set the girl packing or, remove her from the home via a more unofficial way. "You must understand me, my dear Reverend, I am an open-minded woman," she said to him after church services early in May. "I can't send her back to to her family, they are still living in Japan." She admitted she was taken aback by Richard's request for her nanny's hand in marriage. Seth had told her, "He better not be expecting a bloody dowry from me!" They debated for a bit, in the end, she and her husband gave Richard their blessing. They made it clear, however, they didn't want to be involved too much in the whole matter. "I am forward-thinking as I'm sure you know," she reminded the Reverend. "We are pivoting into a new century," Mrs. Rink continued. "It will be love at all costs, regardless of race or creed, mark my words."

The Reverend patted her hand. "I understand completely," he said. He too, wanted very little to do with this rather illicit union. Yet, he was reminded of seminary teachings, that all God's children are equal in His eyes. Even though Sachiko's eyes were so oddly shaped. "It is a wonderful thing that Sachiko was baptized," Reverend Hadivahl said. "And further, it is a fine thing for Christian men and women to marry, regardless of, uh, the circumstances of their birth."

Mrs. Rink proved to be a hypocrite and relished the role of substitute mother-in-law. She fussed behind Sachi all the way from the carriage. "Oh, this dreadful rain," she fretted. "Oh Sachiko, do be careful. Oh my, the rains have never been so bad. Oh dear. Oh watch! Oh, there! There's a dry spot."

Mr. Rink had set down a small step stool to help the ladies to avoid the street water, but it was of no use, it sunk; both women hopped over it.

From a small window in the narthex of the church, Richard watched his bride-to-be tip toe through the water, and as graceful as a dove, safely alighted on the church's upper steps.

Water had crept up to the lower level. The good Reverend was in a fit as the Garden of Gethsemane Fellows reported a foot of water in the Church's basement. They promised to return the following day to bail out the water.

Sachi's cape and hood covered much of her dress, but Richard caught a glimpse of pale blue striped fabric. Sachi was able to get to the top without being as soaked as Mrs. Rink.

"Hey," Robert hissed from behind him, "Get back inside! Don't you know it is bad luck to see your bride before the wedding?"

Richard, heart pounding, took his place at the altar rail. Robert at his elbow, Nathan behind him. Are all grooms this nervous? His father never mentioned this. Surely it was the greatest event in a man's life. The ceremony was all too brief. Tucked into the All-Saints Chapel of the First Presbyterian Church, Richard and Sachi stood side by side. Sachi quietly agreed to love him and cherish him all the days of her life. He produced a small gold band and slid the ring on her tiny finger. He and Robert had gone to Pittsburgh a week earlier to purchase it. He was unable to afford (or wait) for the inscription.

At the very thought of his wedding night, Richard became dizzy.

"Are you alright old man?" asked Nathan. "Looking a bit green about the gills."

Sachi wore a blue striped silk dress, due to a generous supply of cloth from Mrs. Rink. The bell sleeves were inlaid with strips of white linen. In her efforts to be rid of Sachiko, Mrs. Rink became insistent that at least her wedding dress be tasteful. Sachiko was not upset by the woman's overzealous actions. She knew that there was much dishonor committed by this wedding. But Sachi wanted to be Richard's wife with her whole heart. The vows she spoke in a creaky wooden church that smelled of incense and river water, were the truest words she had ever spoke.

"Hai, I will love you."

"Hai, I will cherish you."

"Hai in sickness and in health."

"Until I die."

She had no trepidation speaking these binding words, solemn oaths as heavy as steel. They came off her lips as light as butterflies; so easy. Richard was gentle and caring and determined to be worthy of her. This was admirable. Any man who sought to do this, in any culture, was a treasure to be kept. She was shocked that no other woman saw his character as clearly as she did. His purity of heart was unparalleled.

Sachiko had only to compare Seth Rink to Richard to see the dishonor in one and the honor in the other. In their presence, she could feel both men observing her. Seth with the sickening lust of a troubled soul. Richard with the yearning of a true heart.

Richard stumbled over his vows. He shifted his feet and tried his hardest but he could only stare at Sachi and his mouth went dry. Reverend Hadivahl repeated them several times and coached Richard along. When the final "I do's" were pronounced, there was a general sigh of relief.

The reception, originally designed as a brunch, turned into a luncheon of sorts. Mrs. Rink was terribly put out by the delay of the ceremony. But with great magnanimity set a lovely, albeit, sparse spread on her sideboard.

After the short reception Richard expressed his sincere gratitude to the Rinks, Robert and Nathan as well as Reverend Hadivahl. Richard took his bride, despite the gloomy weather, on a ride in the rented carriage. He had been promised that the clouds would clear up from the liveryman. Sachi parasol was dripping before they reached their destination.

At the top of the hill, overlooking Cambria Iron Works, Mr. & Mrs. Richard Tilridge turned around taking in the view. The valley reminded Richard of a scruffy old dog. Not exactly visually appealing but oddly endearing and loveable. Today, his wedding day, it was gray and misty.

"Richard?"

"Yes, my dear?" Richard responded, thinking, *I can say that to her for the rest of my life. I can call her my Sachi, my dear. She is my wife.*

"The houses are moving."

Richard focused his attention on the homes and buildings that sat at the far end of town. The river seemed to swell and gorge itself of the banks and adjacent land. It bubbled up as an enormous surge of brown liquid. Sachi was right, the houses were moving. Pushed off their foundations and smashing into other houses.

Then they heard the noise. Like the pounding footsteps of a great beast, the splintering, cracking and crashing thundered through the valley.

"Oh, thank God, I found you! Richard, you're not going to believe me when I say this, the dam collapsed!" Robert came at them, falling "out of the door of the incline", running to them in terror. "God help us!" Richard's normally cheerful friend, sank to his knees. "God help us," he sobbed.

The debris collected and slammed against the No. 6 Bridge, stalling the flow of water for a moment, then jammed up behind the bridge. The debris gathered itself and thrust forward and collapsed the Stone Bridge. The wooden debris scored against the ore and coal stockpiles like a giant match. The explosion sent wood and steel flying. And water surged everywhere.

In ten minutes, the town was scoured clean. Businesses and structures were squeezed out of existence. Once the water dissipated miles down the river, residents climbed down off their roofs and got onto drier land. Some found themselves thousands of feet from their original addresses. Others, who had grasped onto debris to keep themselves from drowning, were unrecognizably covered in mud.

Richard and Sachi grabbed Robert and drove the carriage back toward the church. Only there was no church. Only the steps and the bell tower remained. It was as if a mischievous child removed the rest of the building.

Richard got off of the carriage and Sachi, wild with fear, climbed over the edge. Richard clung to her, trying to keep her safe. Smoke filled the air. Sachi struggled out of Richard grasp and scrambled down the hill unconcerned about the dirt and debris.

Richard was behind Sachi, yelling, "What are you doing? No!"

At one point, he saw Sachi on a roof. He beheld the horror on her face, as there were no landmarks, no street signs no way of knowing where anything was or used to be. Using the hills as essential north-south direction, Sachi crawled toward Elm Street and her former employer's home.

Richard caught up to Sachi and he held her as she screamed for Betsy and Eli. She cried out for Mr. and Mrs. Rink. The home of Mr. and Mrs. Rink was no longer. Sachi sank to her knees and wailed. *"Watahis no komodo-tachi,"* over and over again. Richard was by her side and grasped her hand as she began to dig through the fractured wood.

Up above the wreckage, they heard voices.

Betsy and Eli were huddled, muddied, shivering not from cold but from shock.

It was a miracle that Betsy and Eli were alive and not injured. The four of them clung to each other and thanked God for their survival.

Over the next several days, Sachi organized a makeshift orphanage. She collected the motherless children into boys' and girls' tents. She chose the kindest among them to be the leaders. She made sure that they were fed and kept Eli and Betsy close to her. They scanned the valley for arrivals and through the debris saw many new faces eager to help.

Sachi met Clara Barton in a large building, which was set up to be the field hospital for many that were seriously injured since the infirmary had been washed away. Although portions of the infirmary which had smashed against Grumel's General Store were visible.

Sachi admired the small woman's ability to lead without being domineering. Clara made decisions and made them wisely. Barton had taken note of Sachi's make shift orphanage and allowed it to continue. However, Clara Barton was able to enhance the make shift orphanage by providing beds, wash basins and other sanitary supplies. Sachi was only too happy to receive the resources.

In the morning, Richard rose early and left Sachi with Eli, Betsy and the rest of the children. He then joined others at the railway station in order to clear the debris. Richard was made corpsman in charge as many of the leaders had perished or were injured. There was still no word on the Rink's whereabouts. After the third day, Richard presumed them to be dead. One of the main concerns was finding and retrieving survivors from the debris. Richard coordinated and disbursed bands of ten or so men as search and rescue teams in the different areas. In some places men had to hoisted down twenty or more feet to get their feet on the ground at the bottom of wreckage. In the midst of all the mud and debris, Richard suddenly spied something pink sticking between rocks. When Richard dug at the pink item, he couldn't believe his eyes. It was his great grandmother's Queen Conch Shell still intact. Finding the shell was a sign to Richard that he and Sachi would be okay.

A brick warehouse, strong and stable, the lone building to remain standing after the flood, was a makeshift morgue where townspeople visited to find and identify their loved ones. The work was grueling and the weather was humid. Mosquitos and gnats began to bite in earnest. Some men who were fresh from the Spanish-American War spoke of diseases they'd seen in the southern climate. Sleeping sickness and yellow fever that took down entire platoons.

At night, Richard would come home and he and Sachi would fall asleep in each other's arms with Betsy and Eli clinging to them for security. Eli had nightmares and Betsy hadn't spoken since that day. Sachi did everything she could to coax, cajole and finally order the little girl to speak. Betsy only shook her head unwilling to open her mouth.

One night, Betsy screamed out, "Mama!" and Sachi held her close, soothing her with a lullaby:

Hush little one, hush.
I am here for you,
Hush little one, hush
I am dear to you, near to you.
No more tears for you.

Betsy, awake and aware, began to cry out her confession. It was her idea that she and Eli escape the house and find Sachi and Richard to stay with them. "In my house there'd be rooms for all of us to stay." She sobbed. "I didn't want to lose you!" Betsy bullied Eli into coming. He was used to going along on her adventures. Betsy said that by the time they had slipped across the railroad tracks their clothes were badly muddied. Eli balked, "Mama's going to be so cross!" They turned to go back down but the flood waters hit so quickly they clung to each other and soon they found themselves surrounded by water, rapidly rising water! They scrambled to higher floors of the old firehouse as the water rushed in every door and window. They soon found themselves on the roof of the firehouse. The sturdy roof was pinned against the Cambria Ironworks north side. The Ironworks was the only structure recognizable and the only one that remained stable.

"We're safe now children," Richard said. But night after night Betsy cried out in her dreams. And day after day it became clear to him, Sachi and the children that their parents were gone forever.

The fifth evening after the flood, Sachi had come to her limits. At her last count, there were now 102 orphaned children who appeared in her camp. A squabble erupted as the sun went down. They were fighting over sleeping cots. Sachi was at her limits. How to clothe them, feed them, keep them safe from harm and each other.

Just as Sachi put herself between the two children with the loudest voices, a petite woman intervened.

"Well hello children, hello Miss," she said in greeting. "I hope I can help; my name is Clara Barton and I believe we met at the make shift hospital a few days ago." speaking to Sachi. "I wanted to see how you were doing and assess your need for supplies". Three women behind Clara were holding blankets, bed linens and towels for bathing.

The children were silent and looked to Sachi to gauge their reaction to the newcomers bearing gifts. Sachi gave a little nod and accepted their help. The three women expertly divided the children—separating the ones at odds. They distributed the blankets, tucking them into the children's cots and checking the children's hands and faces for signs of disease. With a small gesture, Clara indicated she wanted to speak with Sachi outside the tent so that the children couldn't overhear.

"I came up here to let you know I've set up a humanitarian effort in town and I wanted to offer our help to you" Clara whispered. "Are you faring well? Do you need food?"

Relief washed over Sachi. "Oh, yes, I," she began, but to her shame, she broke into tears.

Dropping her papers, Clara gathered Sachi in her arms. "Oh there, there my dear, haven't we all had a terror." She hugged Sachi tightly. "Are you alone here?"

"No, no, my husband, he's here. He is helping at the Ironworks."

"Would you consider bringing the children into town tomorrow? We have volunteers and so much room. Perhaps some of the children can be reunited with their parents?"

Sachi shook her head. "I think it is unlikely they have living parents."

"I see," Clara paused. "Will your husband be home soon?"

"He comes home late in the evenings," Sachi said.

"Do think of yourself my dear and get some rest," Clara insisted. "We can discuss the needs of the children and enter our tallies in the morning." Clara stood up and retrieved her papers. "Would it be possible for my staff to remain?"

Sachi nodded, grateful for the volunteers' presence.

The following day, Sachi marched the children into the heart of town. Some of them skipped down the hill, excited for a trip anywhere, even to see the town. Their spirits were dampened by the disappearance of their homes.

"Ugh, it smells so bad," said one child, wrinkling her nose. The combination of smoke, fetid water and raw sewage clouded their nostrils.

"Where's my house?" asked another child.

Sachi had no answer. In their children's minds they thought after a few days it would all be restored to its previous orderly state. The only thing any of them could recognize were the train tracks and the iron works. They arrived at Clara's headquarters. It was easy to spot from a long distance. A large red cross was painted on the warehouse.

It came as a happy surprise that two of the children found members of their families. Sachi considered herself fortunate. The dead toll climbed higher every day. Over two thousand men, women and children died. Many family members were never accounted for.

"Have you seen Mr. and Mrs. Rinks?" Sachi inquired. Betsy and Eli clung to her skirt eager for news.

The volunteer looked through her list. "There's no one registered here by that name," she said. "Have you tried the morgues?"

"The morgues?" Sachi repeated. "No, I have not. Please tell me, there is more than one?"

The volunteer informed her that there were four.

Sachi didn't want the children to have to identify their dead parents, it wouldn't do for them to have so many worries. She thanked the volunteer.

Betsy began to sniffle. "Mama, mama."

"Mama, papa," Eli echoed Betsy. He added his mewling to her weeping. "Mama, mama, mama," he moaned.

"And to please excuse me again," Sachi turned back to the volunteer. "Do you have need of assistance to help with the people?"

The volunteer squeaked with joy. "Oh yes! Yes, we do." She ran down the corridor to the mistress of volunteers and gestured to Sachi, Betsy and Eli. Sachi saw the mistress nod and gave the volunteer instructions.

Sachi gathered the children to her. "Listen to me little ones, we need to help. Won't your parents be so proud of you as to help others in such a Christian way?"

Betsy sniffled and nodded, Eli nodded too.

The volunteer returned and ushered them into a large stock room. At one end, a mound of supplies sat in a disordered heap. "We need this to be sorted and stacked," she said, looking at Sachi. "Start here. Linens up top, basins on the bottom. Whatever you can do is greatly appreciated."

For three hours, Sachi and the children folded and stacked. When nurses came in for basins or linens, Sachi allowed the children to retrieve the items. They received many words of praise and encouragement. Sachi was glad for the reprieve. For a few short hours Betsy and Eli focused on folding towels just so, with corners facing in and basins to be counted ten to a stack.

Sachi counted eight days after the flood when the first buzz of mosquitos was heard by her ears. It was another three days after that when the first person, a railroad worker developed the sleeping sickness. Sachi did not understand why they called it the sleeping sickness, no one ever woke up. And many died with their eyes half-opened.

As with many diseases of humans and animals, sleeping sickness or yellow fever preyed upon the most vulnerable –the elderly the already sick or injured and then children. Particularly young children. Sachi, looked at her charges, who were now her children. She made a vow to keep them alive to the best of her ability by using the herbal medicine she knew. She took the children with her (with the exceptions of the ones who were sick and in the care of nurses in the makeshift hospital wards) on foraging trips to the cool forests. June was very hot and fetid.

Sachi collected golden seal and ginseng leaves. She dug up dandelion roots and plucked wild rose hips. The children helped sometimes and they picked black raspberries and wild strawberries to eat. Any berries that went uneaten were saved for dinner. Each night she instructed all the children to drink a small cup of tea. The tea was her infusion made from the leaves she carefully collected, boiled and infused. If a child became feverish Sachi swabbed their foreheads with rags dipped in a mash of strawberry, rose hips and a small amount of whiskey. Richard had purloined a case from the wreckage of the distillery. Neither Sachi nor Richard ever imbibed, so the whiskey for them was medicine.

The yellow fever raged through the broken town. "As if there isn't enough death and destruction," moaned one survivor. "We're served another round?" No sooner did the surge of malaria-stricken bodies pile up than did an arrival of cholera and dysentery. The local water supply and wells had been contaminated. Locals headed into the forest to find fresh spring water.

Sachi boiled all of her water for tea and thus saved herself, Richard and the children from the dreaded disease. She taught the children to relieve themselves in a more hygienic way. Always had a small bouquet of fresh leaves to help rub hands clean.

In one month, the population of Johnstown was cut in half. The town endured heavy rain, catastrophic flooding, malaria, cholera, dysentery and an oppressive heat wave.

Sachi, Richard, Betsy and Eli had also gone through personal transformation. Like the town they became gritty, self-reliant. Sachi became more forceful and protective. She began to think of the children as little butterflies, hard to catch, fluttering without direction but so delicate. She couldn't bear the thought of her charges or any of the children dying.

She knew that children stubbornly resisted things—even those things which were of benefit to them. While sweet cajoling often worked, there was not much time with so many children to spent time singing lullabies or telling stories. It was best to remove their fear quickly and effectively so they would become more compliant. Sometimes it took a sharp word. But Sachi also took advantage of the kinder and older children to help take care of the little ones. One night she told Richard, "I'm so sorry to report that many children are not children any more. They are now little mothers or little fathers."

Betsy and Eli became more secure and they increased their loyalty to Sachi and Richard. Their trust solidified their bonds. They even become comforters to the other children. Sachi saw what a natural leader Betsy was. While Eli was a natural comforter. He also was the one that other children trusted most. They felt safer with Eli.

Richard became less impetuous. He began to listen, realizing that not everyone needed an immediate solution but that they needed someone to listen.

Not one government organization had come to their rescue. The town was abandoned. Only the companies headquartered there were able to gather the resources and manpower to rebuild their investments. At times the railroad companies had to employ security guards to roam the parameters to prevent the desperate from taking advantage of unattended property. First order of business was to restore the roads and simultaneously the rails needed restoration. The restoration/rebuild needed logs and lumber. So once again the mighty oaks came to the aid of humanity as well as the Ginko tree in the making of medicine.

A legal team came from the state to investigate the reason by the dam failed. They went through the gathering of evidence and the painstaking ordeal of interviewing survivors. The state attorney general developed a rather grim timeline that only the South Fork Fishing and Hunting Club (Andrew Carnegie and Henry Clay Frick among its members) and the dam engineers were privy to.

On the day the report was delivered to the interim mayor and his staff, Richard was also advised. There was a crowd at the post office which was now stationed next to the newly constructed rail depot.

The children were up early finishing their chores unaware of the general unrest at the revelation of the details of a disaster that could have been prevented. Before the end of their day, they were able to use the latrine and gathered food for the evening. They returned to their tent on the hill.

Sachi made them wash and get ready for bed, she would tell the children night time stories of dragons who rescued children and happy-ending fairy tales that would lift their spirits so as they slept, they wouldn't have nightmare of crashing muddy waves that drowned their parents.

Richard came home after dark that evening. He apologized. "I'm sorry my dear. I—"

Sachi put a finger to his lips and said "wash" she pointed to a basin of clean water and a small clean towel. In the basin were crushed witch hazel leaves. The pure smell lifted his spirits.

God bless you, he thought, too tired for words.

When he finished washing, she gave him a small bowl of stew. She had made a hearty meal of rice, oats and bits of chicken.

He'd never eaten past nine o'clock and yet at midnight, he ate so quickly, he hiccupped. "Thank you, I—" he began.

Once again Sachi put a finger to his lips. "Sleep," she said. He removed his boots and laid down beside her, a bed never was so downy soft. Now two weeks after the wedding, Richard and Sachi became one flesh. The uniting of husband and wife was soft, gentle and quiet. An inner peace fell over both of them for the first time since the day of the flood.

CHAPTER EIGHT

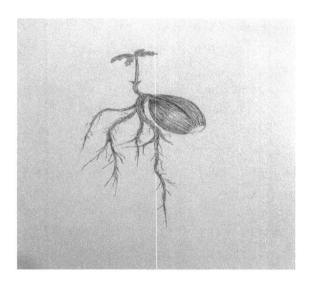

"To exist as a nation, to prosper as a state, and to live as a people, we must have trees."

--Theodore Roosevelt, 1906

Time for a talk with the good pastor.

While Ken and Gilly were glued to the screen, Dan texted Pastor Tom to see if he was free. Pastor Tom texted he'd be free in five minutes.

Ken and Gilly had relocated the sensors and would be engaged in measurements and data for the next couple days.

"They won't even know we're missing," Dan told his mother.

"Why does it take so long?"

"Because it's a massive tree, Mom," Dan said. "They've got to calculate the area of the decay and also ultrasonic machines don't have a long battery life."

Pastor Tom was in his element. He began by giving Dan and Lillian the tour of the exterior of the church and pointed out all the different markings, the keystone, where the church still bore the scorch marks of a fire long ago.

"I'll be honest, I'm kind of here on a mission," Dan confessed. "I love the history of this place and how the tree was a focal point, but we have a post card here we can't explain."

Lillian dug through her purse and produced the postcard. "Do you see what is says? OAK TREE. Basking Ridge, NJ 1944."

"We have no idea what that means," Dan told Pastor Tom. "And it's getting kind of frustrating."

"It came out of my mom's purse. But she's never been here, at least she's never said that she was here. I don't know how she got it. She never told me, never told anyone," Lillian explained. "Can you shed any light on it?"

"Please, let us know if you know anything. Mom's convinced that there's a dead body in the tree," Dan laughed.

"I'm only teasing," Lillian said. "I mean, there isn't one is there?"

"Well," Pastor Tom began. "Yes and no."

1889

As they spent more and more time together, Richard counted his blessings. He didn't understand why no one looked at Sachi the way he did. Her beauty was undeniable. Her manners, her graciousness, her intelligence and her wisdom. Yet, whenever he was in the presence of any of the residents, they grew mute as Sachi approached. The obvious shunning of such a woman of character moved Richard to near despair.

A month after the flood, he and Sachi sat on the small rebuilt porch of the union street home. Sturdy brick and pine unified the survivors' new living quarters. Late in the summer, mosquitoes buzzed all day long, but pine sap from the fresh lumber seemed to dissuade their nocturnal visits. Richard grasped Sachi's hand and apologized for the behavior of people who treated her as though she had some sort of leprosy. He admitted he couldn't quite grasp the motivation.

"You do not see with their eyes," she told him. "To them, I am strange and perhaps evil."

"No! That's not true," he objected.

"I have heard the women talk," she said. "They blame me for so many things."

"Sachi, darling, I know these men and women, they are hardworking, good people. They're just trying to come to terms with this horrible disaster."

"Perhaps. Still, I understand *kyōshin* superstition. Even the wisest in my village, would kill birds because the rain did not fall. They would never stand chopsticks upright in their rice bowls, and they never whistled at night. I am Japanese, I am different and therefore, unlucky. It is easy for them to blame me.

"No, I refuse to listen to this," he cried. He grasped her hand. "I will make it my life's goal to ensure the entire town understands the cause of this disaster. I know, I've heard it and I read it in the newspaper—it was the spillway that no one wanted to fix."

The next day Richard marched into the restored town hall. Bustling with activity, the steps were crowded with people still looking for loved ones, those with landowner disputes and those seeking employment. Richard caught a clerk and requested to see the mayor. He was informed that Mayor Ford had succumbed to malaria. The assistant to the mayor was currently handling official business, but he was cautioned, "Do be quick sir, there's a line half a mile long to see him."

"Oh, I'll be brief," Richard assured the clerk.

After being introduced, the assistant mayor's eyes flew open. "Oh, Richard Tilridge. I have been wanting to see you." He motioned for Richard to sit down. "There's a solicitor who's contacted me about the Rink family. Since your wife was a former employee, I hoped we could meet."

"Certainly, but that's not why I'm here."

I know, I know," he said. "But it so happens the Rink's will and testament has to be executed. The solicitor informed me he is now 30 days without any contact from his clients. He either has to assume they are dead or they must contact him in a period of two weeks."

Richard shifted in his seat. "I, I believe they are gone."

I see, well then may I put you in touch with Mr. Adolphus Morley? He handed Richard a business card. It read: A.S. Morley, Esq. Pittsburgh, Pennsylvania.

"Thank you."

"Now, what did you want to see me about?"

"The cause of this flood sir, had there been any investigation?" It seemed infantile to bring up washerwoman talk with this official, the talk was superstitious gossip and nonsense.

"Yes, we are able to say with certainty that it was the dam by the Sportsman Club at Lake Conemaugh that collapsed due to mismanagement and neglect." stated the acting Mayor.

Even though the newspapers printed the evidence that pointed out the cause for the dam to break leading to the flooding of the town, the gossipers continued to blame Sachi. During a town meeting that Richard and Sachi were attending, a pompous woman, who marched into town meetings on a regular basis, appeared. Normally her disruptions were about the right for women to vote. With her appearance, another woman in attendance whispered loudly, "Good heavens, of all women to be the figurehead for the women's rights movement, why did it have to be her? It's enough to make all women regret the suffragette movement."

The pompous woman was the town's supervisor's wife and she was a force to be reckoned with, like it or not. She looked at Sachi and demanded to know, "Are they your children? They don't even look like you." "Their eyes are not like your eyes," she leveled her gaze at Eli and Elizabeth.

Eli and Betsy clung closely to Sachi, frightened that the woman would do them harm.

Sachi bowed and replied, "Nevertheless they are my children."

"Hmm," the woman grunted. "I highly doubt it."

Gossip had raged around town. Now side comments and conversations traveled through the meeting hall. "How could Mr. Tilridge possible marry a foreigner with all the problems in the world?" ask one gossiper. "We need good old-fashioned families."

"Oh, my yes, couldn't agree more," said another. "Have you seen the pictures from New York? Goodness, all those ugly human weeds coming over here from God only knows where."

"Well, I feel so badly for those dear little children."

"Hmfp if I didn't know better, I'd say they took the children for their inheritance."

"What? No! You think they kidnapped the children?"

"But that would mean they, oh my, killed the parents."

"I think you're all being quite silly, the flood was a horrible thing. Why I was just talking to Mrs. JR Meyers," the gossiper said. "And in our discussion, she had checked the records of the Ladies Guild. We made a large donation to the Red Cross. Mrs. JR Meyers confirms that indeed thousands of people died. She also informed me that many bodies went uncollected."

"What does that mean?"

"It means that it is more than plausible that the Rinks were either washed away or that the children were never able to identify the bodies."

Then a woman with her head held high marched into the town hall meeting and asked to speak with a family supervisor. With all the righteous indignation, she introduced herself as Mrs. George Davies and launched into her favorite subject of the Tilridge family's lack of social harmony. The supervisor caught off guard by the woman's slanderous and unfounded remarks, had the good grace to keep her mouth shut and to allow the woman to keep talking. Give her enough rope to hang herself, she thought.

"Mrs. Davies ended her rant by asking, "Don't you think those children would be in better hands, in the hands of a good family who were never blessed with babies?"

"So, Mrs. Davies, you know these people from your church?" inquired the supervisor.

"Oh, my no, never seen them there."

"You've never invited them to attend?"

"Of course not," she said. Leaning forward she whispered, "They don't look like the type who would attend."

"But you never invited them."

"No."

"Have you ever spoken to them?"

"I never have."

"And you've never welcomed them into the community?"

"I uh," Mrs. Davies stuttered.

"It would have been a Christian thing to do, an act of charity, yes?"

"Well, I—"

"You are a Christian woman, yes?"

Mrs. Davies drew herself up in her chair. "Listen to me carefully those children are in grave danger of—"

"Of what Mrs. Davies? Being taken in, cared for and protected from the likes of you?"

"How dare you!"

"Please leave Mrs. Davies so the town hall meeting can continue with the planned agenda."

After hearing the various comments made by the gossipers, Richard and Sachi felt that they could not remain in the town where their love blossomed. Richard's wanderlust set in as he thought of his father's stories of a Tilridge Farm in Basking Ridge, New Jersey. The town wasn't far from New York City. Surely the population was more diverse and more accepting of people from other countries. Then like being driven by a spirit, they packed their meager belongings and headed for Basking Ridge. Without much trouble, they found and took ownership of the old Tilridge Farm.

The Tilridge family settled into the farm and wanted to be a part of the community. They decided to attend the community church and planned to attend on a regular basis. Richard & Sachi made a point to linger after the service in order to meet Pastor Herman Franz. Pastor Franz noticed that the couple came with children who seemed to be too old for their young faces. Richard Tilridge seemed to be a very thoughtful man. His tiny wife Sachiko, was a lovely Oriental but their children—blue-eyed and blond--looked nothing like either of them. As the children sat in the outer office, Richard and Sachi explained they were guardians of the Rink children since their parents had died in the Johnstown flood. Richard explained he had returned to his family's farm with intentions to cultivate the land and maybe find part time work in the city. He was also able to buy several large tracts of land that abutted the Great Swamp. And the outskirts of the town met up with his land. "We felt that it would be a better place for the children to grow up," he told the Pastor. "Their parents' desire was to have them go to good schools and since this is between the cities of New York and Philadelphia, the children will be exposed to the arts and a fine education."

Pastor Franz was delighted. He gladly registered them with the parish.

He promised he would recommend local schools for the children. "But not too soon," Richard said. "We think," he looked at Sachi. "The children need some time to adjust to a new life here. They've had so much calamity in their life."

Richard worked hard to turn the abandoned Tilridge farm into a thriving and productive enterprise as well as hold a banking job in the city. Sachi, an excellent manager of time and funds, managed the daily operations of the farm along with several hired farm hands. She invested a portion of the earnings into "a rainy-day fund". She remembered all too well how after the Johnstown flood so many people were so destitute there was nothing for them but to live in shelters. Richard and Sachi also devoted a small amount of Elizabeth's and Eli's inheritance into land acquisition for their future. After being on the farm for two years, Sachi became pregnant. Richard and Sachi were thrilled to have their own child. In the autumn of

1891they became parents to a bouncing baby boy, they named him Alan.

Within six years, the Tilridge farm had grown into one of the largest family-operated farms in New Jersey. At 550-acres, Sachi had a lot to manage. Richard rode the train to and from New York City and returned home to find Sachi ready to give him her daily accounting of farm activities.

"Sachi you are a magnate," Richard would tell her. "You're a natural land magnate."

"What does magnate mean?"

"It means you have the head of a great business woman."

She shook her head. "I am only doing what I believe is wise for the children and us."

The only leisure time Richard and Sachi had was on Sunday Mornings before church. They spent the time reading the Sunday newspaper. Their "disappear time" the children called it. It was never to be interrupted. Unless it was of the utmost necessity.

Elizabeth was entering high school, becoming the bubbly, bossy young woman it was always thought she'd become. Eli also became the type of boy Sachi predicted him to be. Quiet and gentle, serious and dedicated to writing and liking journalism. Their youngest was son, Alan, he had dark hair like Sachi and he couldn't sit still. Sachi feared Alan would be their wild child.

"It is so in every family," Sachi assured Richard. "There is always one who is like a running horse."

"You are quite correct, my dear," Richard laughed, watching as Alan careened into furniture. And though he'd fall, he'd pop up and give a big nearly toothless toddler smile. As he was growing up the family all but forgot his Christian surname and called him by his nickname *Yasei-ji*

Near the end of 1896, Sachi was delighted to discover she was pregnant with her second child. She told Richard that a big family was a sign of good fortune.

But their tiny town was raging with Whooping Cough. The disease swept over the state like an ugly, dark wind. Many babies and children were dying of the disease. Every week there was another funeral. It was into this great misery, Martha Tilridge was born.

A tiny perfect, wee little one, the midwife pronounced. Martha was a happy baby. Her older siblings loved to play with her, even Yasei-ji (Alan) peeped into her crib and shook a rattle to make her laugh. Although they were careful, Martha developed a fever and started to have fits of coughing that took many painful moments to subside.

Early in the morning of Martha's sixth month, Richard was awakened by a thump. He jumped out of his bed and ran into the Martha's nursery, only to find Sachi crumpled on the floor.

He gathered her limp form in his arms.

Her eyelids fluttered. "Oh, I must have fainted." She collected her wits and sat up. "Where's Martha?" Sachi reached out toward the crib.

The baby was sleeping peacefully. Her little breaths were even and deep, untroubled by the Whooping cough that Sachi had fretted over only hours before.

"Oh, my dear you are fighting so hard for Martha," Richard cried. "Please take some rest." He half-carried half - pulled Sachi back to bed. "She'll be fine, he urged.

"Martha is sleeping well now."

"But," Sachi began to protest.

"No, hush," said Richard. "Let's not wake her. You need sleep too."

Late that day after a very thorough conversation with Elizabeth, Richard looked into hiring a private nurse for Sachi. Richard was certain that Martha had caught the deadly Whooping Cough disease and there was not much he could do. One doctor told him it was highly unlikely that Martha would survive another month. He worried over Sachi. She was wearing herself down. He had asked her in the following days why she refused the nurses help. "Why not allow the nurse watch Martha through the night so you can get some rest?" "She is me," Sachi said. "This little girl child was unfortunate—she will die. This is what they told my mother about me. I am fighting for Martha as my mother fought for me."

The doctor's fears were realized when Martha had a coughing fit that didn't subside. Martha turned blue from coughing and died in her mother's arms. Martha died at the age of 7 month 15 days.

Sachi sank into a depression. Martha's death felt as her own dying. In her childhood she remembered the two funerals of her Buddhist family members and the *tohba* that stood like wooden feathers. She took limbs that had fallen from the Great Oak Tree and wrote words in Sanskrit, thinking that they would bring Martha back—she poured water and left small cakes. Nothing stirred, even the Great Oak Tree stood still. Martha was not coming back.

Every night Richard would gather Sachi in his arms and tell her, "I love you; I need you." He never knew if Sachi heard. Every morning Richard would leave to go to work, check with his foreman on the farm and leave for New York City. When he returned, Sachi hadn't gotten up. Elizabeth did her best to comfort Sachi with help from the nurse, she'd spoon a few sips of broth into Sachi's lips. And pester her to eat some porridge.

Sachi's eyes sank further and further into her skull. Richard prayed like he never prayed before. He lit candles, visited Martha's grave, begged for prayers from the assistant pastor.

"God is not a divine magician," the assistant sniffed. "It's not as if I have a special prayer for your wife. She is grieving."

"Where is Pastor Franz?"

"He's tending to his flock," snapped the assistant. "I haven't seen him in two days. Your child isn't the only one that died."

It was the nurse that gave Richard the hope he clung to. "Do as you are doing," she counselled him. "Tell her how much you love her and need her, speak to her, and never ever ignore her, even though she may ignore you."

A month after Martha's death, Sachi came back to the living. Richard came home one night, after wrangling a particularly difficult overseas account. And he heard crying. He searched for Sachi and found Elizabeth in Martha's nursery with Sachi weeping in her lap.

"There, there," she was saying to Sachi. "Don't cry. Oh look, here's Richard!"

Richard picked up Sachi and carried her back to their bedroom.

When she stopped weeping, she said, "I am sorry to behave so badly."

"Never apologize for grieving over our beautiful Martha."

On the first anniversary of Martha's death, Sachi paid a visit to the small grave stone in the Tilridge section of the cemetery. Her daughter's small marker was adorned with colorful flowers, it stood out in comparison to the other grave markers. Small flat wooden sticks, in the manner of Japanese symbolic blessings flanked the marker. Sachi knew that to anyone else, these decorations would look silly, inappropriate for the somber plot of land. All of a sudden, Sachi heard the soft sound of a song coming from the Great Oak Tree and she felt a warm mist circle her and it comforted her. Sachi couldn't wait to tell Richard about what happened at Martha's grave. Then Richard told Sachi about all of the stories and legends of the Great Oak Tree that were passed down in his family from one generation to another. He thought of his great grandmother's Queen Conch Shell and wondered if it was time to bury it on Sarah Tilridge's grave. Richard also thought about what his Wall Street boss told him at their last meeting in the office. His boss told him that the Buttonwood Agreement of May 17, 1792 was signed by 24 Stock Brokers at 68 Wall

Street, New York. The Brokers sat outside under a Buttonwood Tree for the signing of the agreement. "Did the Buttonwood tree have a soul like the Great Oak Tree?" Richard wondered.

Sachi's spirit for living and running the farm returned. She nurtured Alan, her *Yasei-ji* and she became pregnant with twins. In the fall of 1898 she gave birth to twin boys which pleased Richard.

One frosty night, a family came to plead their case with Richard and Sachi. They were headed west as jobs and opportunities were drying up and they planned to join the father's relatives in Minnesota. The father explained how their middle child, Axel, didn't want to go west. Axel wanted to stay near the Tilridge Farm since it was part of his heritage. "What do you mean his heritage?" asked Richard in shock. Axel's father explained that his wife was a descendant of Jeremy and Sarah Tilridge. Axel's full name was Axel Tilridge Mars. Axel than asked if he could stay and live with Richard and his family. Axel was tall, thin, strong and 15 years old. "Please let me stay," begged Axel.

Richard and Sachi were shocked yet pleased to learn about a lost branch of the Tilridge family tree. Richard turned to Sachi, "Can we afford to feed another mouth?" Sachi said yes, but he will have to work hard and sleep in the carriage house. The upper floor of the carriage house served as a roughed out living quarters. The Mars's were reluctant to leave Axel behind. They assured Axel that if things didn't work out between him and the Tilridge's, he could join them in Minnesota.

Axel was happy to be finally on the Tilridge Farm but sad not to be with his parents and siblings. He was a very hard worker albeit sullen at times. He kept to himself and only spoke at the end of the day at supper. He never complained about working at the Tilridge farm. Somedays when he was out in the barn milking, he would say to the Holsteins, "One day this will be mine." The cows would moo their support.

Axel was taught to read and write English by necessity leading to minimal ability to read and write. His limited ability to read and write became a problem when Richard purchased two tractors built with gasoline-powered internal combustion engines for the farm. The operational manual was written in English. Although it was filled with many diagrams, it still needed the operator to be literate in English.

Elizabeth teased Axel. She discovered while he was fluent in speaking German and English he couldn't read or write very much in either language. "Now how on earth will you succeed in reading that thing?" she said pointing to the owner's manual. "You have to be able to read and write well in at least one language."

"And not just that manual, how will you get ahead in the world?" The next day Elizabeth handed Axel one of her grammar books from school. He had never seen let alone owned a textbook, or a book of any kind. "You can't stay here forever," stated Elizabeth.

"Why not?" he challenged. "I am happy here."

"Hah!" taunted Elizabeth, spell 'happy'."

"F-A-R-M." he retorted.

For once she was speechless.

He felt like he won a major victory.

Whenever Axel and Elizabeth were together, they tried to surprise each other in a game of wits. Elizabeth usually got the upper hand. Axel however, had the glorious upper hand once in a while. Axel became proficient in reading and writing English with Elizabeth's excellent tutoring.

Axel Tilridge Mars fell head over heels in love with Elizabeth Jane Bolton Rink. As a nearly grown man, it came to him in slow and steady drips. Their childish games became more serious; less about teasing and more about testing. His heart had certainly been nearly broken by Elizabeth's childish game playing by bringing home suitors and dangling them in front of Axel.

John Forish was a cousin of a cousin of the Astors, and as wealthy as the Rinks once were. Elizabeth reminded everyone after being told she would have to delay her college education, "the Astor women never delay their college education." Her pouting lasted as long as a summer rain storm. Her good heart reigned supreme and she agreed to wait until next year to attend Princeton University. Besides helping Sachi with the twins and Alan, she mercilessly teased Axel.

One night, she timed her good night to John in front of the large porch on the Tilridge estate just as Axel was coming in to have supper with the family.

"Good night, John," Elizabeth said loudly and offered her check to John.

John pecked the rosy skin and said, "Goodnight Liz."

Axel took exception to the brazen peck on her cheek and the use of a nickname. Eli would call her Dizzy Lizzy frequently to irritate her. Elizabeth dismissed her brother, and privately informed Axel that as woman of the new century, she should take on a new "persona." Axel had taken her news with a grain of salt. He believed that much of her "stretching her boundaries" was a ploy to see how much she could get away with. She was still called Elizabeth by Richard and Sachi. She still had a curfew and she still wasn't permitted anywhere in public with a man without a chaperone.

When John left, Elizabeth could see Axel approaching. She also knew without even seeing his face, she had embarrassed him beyond measure.

"Oh, hello Axel, I didn't see you there," she said airily.

He ignored her lie and asked, "Why are you ashamed of your name?"

"What? Oh that. I told you I am a woman with a new persona and therefore a new name."

"You are still the same. It makes no sense, Elizabeth."

"I don't expect it to make sense to anyone unable to look forward with new vision about women's roles," Elizabeth taunted him.

"I don't need to see the future to know the role you'll play with that ruck."

The slap caught them both by surprise. Axel pressed his hand to his cheek. The sting was a catalyst for his kiss. He grabbed Elizabeth by the shoulders and pressed his lips against hers.

Elizabeth pulled away first and staggered up the stairs.

Axel, ashamed of his behavior, went hungry that night. It would not be the last time.

The next morning, a more demur Elizabeth mumbled a greeting to Axel as they sat down to a breakfast with Sachi, Richard, Eli, Alan, and the twins. Sachi saw Axel's face. Never had a man so ardently given himself away. Elizabeth was in love with Axel since he came to them as a young man but wouldn't admit it. Sachi approved of the match. They would fight and struggle, but they would not want anyone else. Richard also approved of the match.

Richard and Sachi confided in Axel and revealed to him how and when Elizabeth and Eli would receive their inheritance. Richard explained that when Elizabeth reached 25 years of age, she was to receive her half and Eli would receive his half when he turned 23. "Eli is a better money manager than Elizabeth. And after all, it is a male's responsibility to provide and manage a family's finances." Richard stated and then catching Sachi's look, added "Men should include their wife when making financial decisions." Sachi smiled at Richard. Then Richard continued, "You must understand, you, Sachi and I are the only ones who know this." "The money is all they have left from their parents, everything else was washed away in the Johnstown Flood." "Their money is in a Trust Fund at the bank invested in stocks and bonds."

"You can trust me not to say anything to anyone," Axel promised.

"Axel, I also know that you are very fond of Elizabeth. I approve of your match."

When Elizabeth turned 23, Axel and her where married. It was a lovely wedding held at the church. The wedding ceremony was held under the Great Oak Tree. Both Richard and Sachi thought they heard the Great Oak Tree signing softly in the background. The spirit among the wedding guests was cheerful and happy. After the wedding ceremony, a picnic lunch was provided for the guests in the church's picnic grove. The branches of the Great Oak Tree loomed over the grove and provided shade and a cool breeze.

Axel and Elizabeth remained on the Tilridge Farm for two years after their wedding. They were very happy helping Richard & Sachi on the farm. As usual, the young couple wanted a place of their own. Axel's parents never made it to Minnesota but settled in what his parents called the most beautiful valley they had ever seen. The valley was home to a small town named Pine Grove in Pennsylvania. The town was small but there was a great deal of farm land with good soil and water. The Mars's begged their son to bring his wife to Pine Grove and set down roots in the beautiful valley. So when a farm came up for sale near Axel's parents, Elizabeth and Axel made plans to visit Axel's parents and check out the farm.

CHAPTER NINE

"And into the forest I go, to lose my mind and find my soul."
--John Muir, 1892

Dan's eyes popped open. "Wait, what do you mean, 'yes and no.'?"

"Look, I'm not a tree expert," Pastor Tom apologized. "I'm just a church guy. And I've got about 200 years plus worth of church records. More than just baptisms, weddings and deaths. The gals at the library have archived all of it. And they're uploading it on the National Library of Congress database. The BR Photo shop is scanning all the photos onto CDs. It's taken about four years."

"That's impressive," said Lillian. "What kinds of images? Anything that looks like the postcard?"

"Oh yeah, sure, this tree is pretty internationally famous," Pastor Tom said. "Pretty proud of how the postcards have gotten all around the world."

"That's all fine and good but it still doesn't help us explain why this card—especially one published around war time— would have gotten into my grandmother's purse."

"One thing at a time," Pastor Tom paused. "First, to your question about the yes and no answer I gave you."

"Oh, okay, let's hear this one."

"There's the possibility that in the roots of the tree there may be, um, dead bodies."

"I knew it!" shouted Lillian.

"So, the 'no' part of that is if there are any dead bodies 'in' the tree it would have to be at the root level."

"Why do you say that?"

"Well, about sixty years ago when we moved the cemetery to the back there—we had to exhume the bodies. It was a dicey task, I'll tell ya. The Trenton medical examiner was here with her team. Experts from Princeton's forensic science department came out too. They identified some of the bodies, had to bury them in new caskets. Many of the people buried were poor and interred in simple pine box caskets. They breakdown in ten years. But there were three they just couldn't dig out."

"Why not?"

"The roots wouldn't let them go."

"The roots also had grown in and around some kind of sea shell."

1907

It was in the spring of 1907 when Axel & Elizabeth went to visit his parents and check out the farm. Axel's parents were so happy to see their son and Elizabeth. They couldn't believe how they had matured into fine young adults. Axel's parents did everything they could to entice Axel & Elizabeth into to buying the 200 hundred acre farm next to them. Axel loved the barn and Elizabeth loved the farmhouse and both of them loved the valley with the mountains on each side and the many streams that ran through it. They decided to purchase the farm using some of Elizabeth's inheritance. Now the hard part was to return home to Basking Ridge and inform their family there that they would be moving to Pennsylvania. Everyone (Richard, Sachi, Eli, Alan and the twins) was saddened by the news. They tried to be happy for them and wished them success with their new undertaking.

Prior to moving to Pine Grove, the family held a farewell party for Axel and Elizabeth with their friends and neighbors. It was a joyous and a somber event rolled into one. Richard decided that it was time to bury Great Grandma Tilly Tilridge's Queen Conch Shell on Sarah Tilridge's grave. Jeremy's grave was on Tilly's right side and Martha's grave was on her left side. Once again the Great White Oak Tree seemed to be softly singing a song while Richard buried the Queen Conch Shell. A mild breeze danced through the Great Oak and once again a mist appeared and it surrounded the family. Richard felt that it was a sign that at long last the spirits of Sarah and Tilly were joined and they were rejoicing. "Why had he waited so long to fulfill the promise he made to his father?" he seemed to be asking the Great Oak Tree.

Farming was different in Pine Grove and Axel and Elizabeth had to make many adjustments to their ways of living and farming. The farm was smaller than the Tilridge Farm and the main goal was to raise cows for milk and butter and steers for meat. The grains that were grown were used to feed the livestock not sold to buyers like in New Jersey. They had more foul (chickens, turkeys and geese) and even fruit trees.

In the second spring of being in Pine Grove, Elizabeth gave birth to a round faced, dark haired boy. They named him Harrison Eli Tilridge Mars. The families were beyond happy for the new addition. Richard, Sachi, Eli, Alan and the twins traveled to Pine Grove to see the baby. It was so good to have a baby in the family again. Eli was honored that his sister named the baby partly after him. Richard & Sachi were thrilled to be grandparents, they liked the farm and the valley.

In no time at all, baby Harrison (Harry) was toddler Harry and Elizabeth, of all people, insisted that Harry learn to speak English and German. The little boy was bilingual before he went to school.

Axel worried that his son would be treated differently if he spoke German in school. His worries were for naught since there were Irish, Italians, Germans and Dutch children in his grade. Most of the children's parents were refugees and immigrants who were desperately trying to find something better in the New World.

1914

In 1914, the fiery Pastor Herman Franz of the First Presbyterian Church in Basking Ridge warned his congregation that, "Although we are far removed in time from the horrors of slavery, there is much to be desired about the acceptance of the Negro and foreigner in our land—even our own town. Let us not forget the immigrants among us who have fled oppression to seek a better life."

Pastor Franz observed the shunning of Italian and Irish immigrants in the town. Though none of them attended his church—all were solidly Catholic, he couldn't help but feel for them as their status of outcasts. It seems as if their humanity was superseded by an unhealthy distrust of the foreign tongues and faces. Pastor Franz was chagrined that his flock treated some brethren unkindly instead of being the truly Good Samaritan.

On one such occasion he witnessed a member of the men's guild shove an elderly Italian woman who was combing through the cemetery gathering chestnuts.

"Get out," shouted the man. "This is hallowed ground and no place for the likes of you!"

Pastor Franz determined to clarify the teaching of the church, sat down on a Saturday evening determined to right the wrongs by penning a golden rule treatise. With a holy frenzy, he scratched out page after page. Some he re-read and disliking the words, crumpled them, tossing them to the floor. He wrote past dusk. At midnight, he doused his lamp.

In the morning, in keeping with the rebellious spirit of his ancestors, he nailed his, "All men are equally loved by Almighty God" to the Great Oak Tree. He placed it just so, in the direct line of vision of those who would be looking out the windows when he began his sermon.

And anyone who visited the cemetery to tend to the graves of their family, would also see it. The world was changing so fast he warned his flock. There are so many people of different countries coming to our shores and we must meet them with open arms, there is so much room here for them to settle.

Pastor Franz remembered how in 1884 he was bolstered by the gift of the Statue of Liberty. It was gifted to the United States by the French. Words associated with "The Lady" stayed with him: *Give me your tired, your poor, your huddled masses yearning to breathe free.* He had read reports of masses of people flocking to Ellis Island to be quarantined and then released into America. The newcomers were a cause for fear for some people, but for Pastor Franz it was a thrill. It meant the country was growing and that the country was truly blessed by God.

One morning Richard stood up. "No!" he cried. "War has been declared in Europe." He read the front page aloud to Sachi. "The Archduke Franz Ferdinand and his wife Sophie of Austro-Hungary were assassinated in Sarajevo on 28 June 1914." The assassination led the Austro-Hungarian Government to declare war on Serbia. Then on 3 August Germany declared war on Russia.

Sachi bowed her head. Of course, she knew nothing of the workings of international politics. But listening to Richard read the paper, she knew if a person killed a leader, an army would march against their country. She was not surprised that leaders of countries squabbled over boundaries. She know the working men would be sent to battles while the women were abandoned, left to fend for themselves. From the grumblings of the men at the Church, it sounded that inevitable this war declaration would come to involve America. Sachi's main concern was how this would affect her family.

Sachi would fine out soon enough.

Pastor Franz's family in Belgium were some of the first victims of the war. The pastor had received a letter from his family expressing great concern. A month after the assassination, the Belgian government had soothed its inhabitants by telling Germany and the world that if war came it would uphold its historic neutrality. The pastor's family was not fooled. They didn't trust Germany. Weeks later the Belgian government mobilized its armed forces at the end of July. In a week, Germany invaded Belgium and many innocent people were killed. Pastor Franz's cousins were among the dead. A telegram was delivered to the pastor's residency informing him of the family deaths.

His grief was immeasurable. Grabbing a knife, he meant to do himself harm, but a flutter of pages still nailed to the Great Oak Tree - his "All men are equally loved by Almighty God" treatise mocked him from the cemetery. At first he was angry with seeing the papers and then he took the words he wrote to heart. He put the knife down and fell to his knees. He asked God to forgive him and started to pray for the safety of remaining family member in Belgium. He continued to preach his "All men are equally loved by Almighty God and added that it's the sinful acts of men that displeases God." He continued to encourage church members to open their arms and welcome the newcomers to Basking Ridge.

Mrs. Graham Everett, a friend of Sachi, was very much moved by Pastor Franz's words and she began a community fund to help newcomers in need of housing, food and clothing. She also started a welcome committee at the church. The committee members helped newcomers with language problems, enrolling children in school, banking and other issues the newcomers faced. Some just needed someone to talk to.

Sachi and Ellen (Mrs. Graham) discussed the recent news events of the wars in Europe.

"It's all so horrible," Ellen concluded. "What do you think?"

"I think we should prepare," Sachi said.

"Prepare for what?

"For the men in this town to be in the war."

"Why would you even say that?" Ellen was shocked.

"Because this war will touch everyone, no one will escape."

Sachi was right. In less than a year, Germany sank Great Britain's *Lusitania*. It was an unprovoked and outrageous crime. A year later, the United States had danced the diplomatic dance with Germany. Signing the Sussex Pledge in 1916, Germany promised not to fire upon non-military vessels. But a year later with diplomacy failing. The United States declared war on Germany on 6 April 1917.

1917

Richard was too old to enlist. Men between the ages of 21 and 30 were required to register for military service. Eli had just turned 31 and Axel was 33. Sachi and Elizabeth relaxed their fears of having to send them off to war.

Back in Pine Grove, Axel and his friends who were in their thirties thought that it was an honorable thing to enlist in the army. After putting Harry to bed, Elizabeth sat with Axel and spoke to him about enlisting. "I do not want you to leave, what if you are killed? What will I do without you?"

"I feel I must fight for our country." "You are a very smart and capable woman, Elizabeth. I will miss you and I plan to come home to you." "Harry is 8 years old and he along with my parents and sisters next door will be able to help you with the farm."

What Axel said was true. She managed the household and helped Axel with the farm work.

"Maybe it's because I'm afraid of losing you," she confessed. "I'm afraid of letting you go."

"You must return," Elizabeth said. "I will pray for your safety." "My love will return you to me."

Three days later, Axel Tilridge Mars enlisted in the army. He trained briefly at the old Carlisle Barracks, learned how to shoot a Colt-Browning and wrote letters to Elizabeth every day. He was shipped off to France. Crowded aboard the Queen Mary, he was proud he didn't get seasick like so many other men.

His luck nearly ran out at the Battle of Amien. His outfit was an amalgam of U.S., Canadian, Australian and British forces. Digging trenches, the men hunkered down in close quarters. Early in the morning of August 8, Richard's unit was given the orders to advance. They were to accompany tanks and go on the offensive.

"Bloody early in the morning for a walk isn't it, Colonel?" one soldier asked.

"Never too early, just make sure you're back for tea."

The unit laughed, but as they marched, they grew silent. Ears strained to pick up the noise. And it came with ferocity. Explosions happened with every other heartbeat. Tanks hammered the German line. In two miles, Richard's unit was face to face with German soldiers. The units threw themselves on the ground, fired their rifles and lunged forward. Some men never got up. Axel advanced, doing his best not to step on bodies.

At one point, his line was jammed against a low ridge. A British soldier popped his head above the embankment and relayed his observation. "They're on retreat, we've caught them by surprise." As if to counter the information an explosion happened so close to their position, the entire line was nearly buried in a shower of dirt and debris.

"Now!" the commanding officer took the poor visibility as an advantage to fling his troops into the fleeing Germans. The Fourth Army flooded over the ridge firing as they moved. Axel hunched forward bending over to avoid the shelling that was now going over their heads and blowing up holes behind them.

They were met with a volley of fire. The Germans had ceased their retreat and were digging in on higher ground.

Axel knelt to reload his rifle and caught a bullet through his shoulder. It spun him around and flattened him on the ground.

"Aw bloody hell," a British solider yelled as he fell grabbing his thigh. He looked over at Richard. "Hey mate, you still with us?"

"Yes, yes, I'm wounded, shoulder," Axel panted. He gathered the bottom end of his uniform and jammed it into the wound.

"Not to worry, there's a medic on his way, I just passed him over by…"

Axel passed out before he ever knew where the medic was.

Three weeks later, he was patched up and sent home to Pine Grove. He was horribly seasick for the return trip. Elizabeth met him and uncharacteristically cried as she greeted him. "Welcome home my honorable husband. Never go away again!" Axel was discharged from the army with honors and World War I ended on 11 November 1918.

CHAPTER TEN

"We are born believing. A man bears beliefs as a tree bears apples."
                                                      --Ralph Waldo Emerson, 1832

Dan shook his head. "Roots holding onto a body?" He looked at his mother. "Uh, no, never happened."

"Hey, I said I was no tree expert," Pastor Tom reiterated. "The team exhuming the bodies couldn't get all the caskets from underneath the roots."

"It's so sad to think there was a person who'll never be buried in a proper ceremony," said Lillian.

"No, no, I'm sure who ever it was had a proper ceremony. Judging by the dates, it might have been someone who died from the Spanish Flu. There were quite a few buried in the cemetery.

"Oh, how sad, Lillian said "How old were they?"

1919

At the end of the Great War, the world suffered more deaths by the Spanish Flu Pandemic. The spread of the Flu was uneven in the United States and the little town of Pine Grove was not hit with the virus.

While Axel fought in World War I, Harry went to school and helped his mother tend the farm.

School for some was a way for the parents to keep their wild children off the streets. Education was for many a path to becoming civilized. Especially the boys. They were not stupid but incredibly mischievous. It took a very alert and agile teacher to keep the class on track at the George Washington Elementary.

Before the school bell rang in elementary school, Harrison, Harry to his peers, was thrilled to hear different languages. For his ears it was like a tasty dish with different spices that blended so well. Like an experienced chef, he was able to pick out the spices and their contribution to the dish which was the school yard.

He heard different dialects of Italian—Sicilian and Roman. He understood that not all Germans spoke alike. Some of the immigrant children came from the region of Alsace-Lorraine. It sounded to his ears, almost as lilting as French. He could tell the difference between the Polish and Czech.

Harry listened well to the school yard altercations, and went home repeating his new international vocabulary of words and phrases. In less than three months, Harry knew how to insult people in five different languages.

But in the classroom, it was always English. English grammar, English literature, English culture. He wondered if the students from other countries were upset that no other language was taught or that no other literature was discussed. There was the odd reference to classics like Plato, Homer, Aristotle, but it was as if no other country produced literature. To his teacher, it didn't seem to matter. The students enjoyed learning. For a while, the education elevated them from beyond their poverty. Even though they struggled with words that didn't make sense, they loved the stories of Mark Twain and O. Henry.

As Harry advanced in grade levels, his interest grow for reading and literature. Harry inherited his love for reading from his grandfather George Mars who was an English teacher. Harry went on a small hunt for stories in the romance languages. He found dark fables of the Grim Brothers. He discovered the political machinations of Machiavelli and Dante's *Inferno*. He dabbled into French poetry and studied the dangerous writings of Lenin.

In order to immerse himself in the language, Harry needed to learn a little more—music. Piano was out. His mother and father would never buy something that large. He pondered over the different instruments. Even looking into the instrument rental program at school. Most of the instruments available were beat up trumpets or bugles from the Great War. Grandpa Tilridge had a ceremonial bugle. It was nestled in a lined velvet case which he never opened, save once a month to clean and polish it. He played a few selections for Harry, but they were only the military warbling calls for charge, advance, retreat, and taps. None of which enhanced Harry's love of music, language or foreign culture.

1923

To Harry's great good fortune when he was 14, he was taken to New York City as a Christmas treat. Stuffed into an old Packard, with his cousins Trena and Emily, he bundled his ears against their chattering. They were taken to New York by older, wiser Uncle Alan. It was supposed to be a day of fun for the teenagers. They were treated to the sights and sound of the bustling city. It was the "Roaring Twenties" and seeing so many women dressed in the "Flapper Style" was quite a sight for the teenagers from rural Pennsylvania.

Harry wasn't impressed by the buildings. They looked like concrete beehives. Not a blade of grass. "Oh, there are acres of grass in Central Park!" Alan told Harry. Still, from what Harry saw, the city didn't have a particular style. The whole place was noisy, crowded and smelly. Still, it had an energy, he couldn't deny.

He begged his Uncle to take side trips to Chinatown, Hell's Kitchen or even a Bavarian biergarten. He was turned down.

"You're too young," came the response. "I'll take all of you to Times Square. It's the bees' knees!" The girls were thrilled.

Harry was not. He decided to make his own side trip.

Harry made a turn onto Mulberry Street and found himself in a new country. Overloaded with aromas of garlic, sweat and wet rags. Above him, the buildings were connected by laundry lines with clothes, it reminded him of pennants of a baseball teams. Then he heard a man and a woman fighting and off of the second floor came an accordion. For a moment it hung suspended on a sole strand of clothesline. Then it toppled down to the street below.

Harry rushed to catch the falling instrument and managed to catch it before it hit the ground. In the process his knees met the cobblestones below and ripped holes in his pants. A dark-haired woman—the accordion tosser—looked out the window, puzzled. Was she disappointed she didn't hear a crash?

"Hey!" She yelled at Harry.

He jumped to his feet, cradling the accordion like a new born kitten.

"Buoan fortuna per tutto!" she yelled after him.

He turned out of the side street and headed for Broadway. Alan had said they were going to Times Square which was now blocks away. He picked up his pace. How did he get so lost so quickly?

Minutes later, a panting Harry found his frantic uncle and seething cousins. Emily looked like she was ready to skin him alive.

"What in the blazes happened to you?" Uncle Alan yelled. "Oh, your mother is going to have a cow! I promised her nothing would happen to you kids. I practically swore on a stack of Bibles."

"I got this," breathed Harry, panting, but joyous, holding up his new treasure.

"What is it?"

"An accordion."

"Oh no! Did you steal it?"

"No," answered Harry. "They were going to toss it. I just saved it from the street," he answered honestly.

Harry came home and much to his parents' surprise, he began practicing "Ladies of Spain" as well as a few Dutch lullabies. He mastered *"You are My Sunshine."* It was his morning favorite and he played that at the beginning of each school day.

Axel shook his head. "How do you explain that?" He looked up at the ceiling, while Harry was in full throttle of *"Peek-a-boo Waltz"*.

Elizabeth had no words. "Well, he likes music."

His cousin Trena often visited and hated the accordion. She was a child of the 20's and loved everything boater hat and ukulele. She'd tell Harry that she was fine if he wanted to practice, but to do so in another county. Or she'd yell, "Stop" and loudly slam the door to his room. Her opinion of talent was never identified. But her raging disapproval of his choice of instrument was never a secret. It only made him play louder.

"Do you know what I think of your accordion?"

"I don't care," he responded packing it away in a small storage box he'd made of pine. He had cannibalized an old boot chest using its rusty hinges for a swing-open door.

"I think it sounds like someone ran over an organ with a tractor."

He stuck his tongue out at her.

She responded in kind.

1925

Pastor Narberth, who replaced Pastor Franz, traveled to the Telridge Farm to see Richard.

"Well, this is a surprise," Richard said as he shook the Pastor's hand.

Sachi bowed in greeting and welcomed the tall thin darkly clad Pastor into her home. She remembered him from church and the cemetery. Pastor Christopher Narberth was very kind to her and kept Martha's grave neat and tidy—unlike his assistant. Pastor Narberth tended all the graves—pulling weeds and keeping the tunneling creatures away. She knew he cared for the living as much as he cared for the dead.

"I had to make this trip to see you," the Pastor took off his hat. "You are one of most successful member of the church. I must say that I am very impressed with the beauty of your farm and I should have visited sooner."

"Thank you," said Richard. "I'm rather proud of this farm. We're on the grain exchange and are actually feeding many of the countries that were devastated by the Great War."

The pastor accepted a small cup of tea from Sachi. "Well, I'm hoping you can help me," he said after a while.

"I hope I can too," replied Richard.

"You know the Great Oak Tree at the church? I don't know what to do," he sighed. "There is decay in the tree and I am not sure how to save it."

Richard paused. "May I ask, without offense, why do you want to save it?"

"I'm not sure myself," he answered honestly. "In these days after the war, we need a reason to hope, a reason to smile—to remember the simple things. The world is changing so quickly and not in a good way. People long for the old days. Myself as well. And the Great White Oak Tree is a constant, a reminder that no matter how absurd things may get, they can count on the tree to be there."

"I know nothing about trees, dear pastor, I work in investments and here on the farm not logging."

"I wanted to approach you first," he admitted. "Of all my congregants, you have a reputation for getting things done."

Richard laughed. "I'm not the kind of go-getter I used to be," he said. "But I am persistent."

"That's exactly what I need." The pastor went on to explain that while replacing the roof on the bell tower, the workman, at a certain vantage point, looked down at the tree. He told me that the center appeared brown. "The word they used was 'rotted'."

"Oh no," Richard said. "That's not good. Has anyone gotten a closer look?"

"Not yet," the pastor said. "That's where you come in."

"I can't climb up into the tree," Richard protested.

"No, no, I'm not asking you to do that," Pastor Narberth said. "I am asking you to collect a group of men to assess the damage and to see, if possible, what's necessary to heal the tree."

Despite his deflections, Pastor Christopher Narberth was certain Richard was the right person for the job. In what amounted to be a divine mission, Richard spoke to a number of lumber men and tree experts. He made an appointment to visit with the more learned tree men at the botany department of Rutgers University. He invited the department chair to come see the Great White Oak Tree and hopefully offer a remedy.

Richard and his team of very able Basking Ridge men were rebuffed.

"The tree is old," they dismissed in a letter to Richard. "Probably been dying for a number of years." They ended the letter with a rather snobbish head wag. "Not worth our time."

Richard traveled into town and read the letter to the team of townspeople who dubbed themselves "Friends of the Great Oak." They were all in agreement that they'd invite a team of experts from Princeton University.

"And if they say no?" Richard asked. "What then?"

The consensus was to continue to search until they found someone who could offer a solution as to how to save the tree. "We must keep trying to find a way to save the Great Oak," concluded Pastor Narbeth.

"We have no money or funds to compensate anyone for this," Richard argued. It was Friday and he was ready to go home to Sachi. He was feeling his age these days. When he arrived home, the house was quiet and peaceful. The twins were still in college working on their PhD degrees, Alan was outside taking care of the farm, Axel and Elizabeth were in Pine Grove and Eli married the love of his life and lived next door. Alan was happy on the farm and pleased that his parents made him a partner in the Tilridge Farm. In time Alan took over the leadership of the Friends of the Great Oak group. He felt a close bond to the Great Oak Tree. Richard found that his work and the farm didn't allow him enough time to head the committee. Under Alan's leadership the Friends of the Great Oak had a plan that would save the Great White Oak Tree. Eli still working in Journalism, read an article how folks in a small village in France saved a tree from dying. Eli gave the article to Alan and Alan shared it with the group. The Friends of the Great Oak group decided to try what the France did. The method involved using tar paper and cement. First they lined each cavity, there were almost a hundred cavities throughout the Great Oak, with the tar paper and then the cavity was filled with cement. The Friends of the Great Oak added the installation of iron rods into the crotches for support and to keep large branches from splitting from the tree.

1929

May 31st and it was Richard and Sachi's 40th Anniversary. The entire family had gathered at the Tilridge Farm to celebrate the occasion. Everyone was in a festive mood and it was so good for the family to be together again. The family ate until they couldn't eat another bite, they played games, they sang as Harry played his accordion and they talked and talked. They retold the stories of the Tilridge family and the legends of the Great Oak Tree. Alan also gave an update on the progress of trying to save the Great Oak.

Then as the weekend was coming to an end, Richard gathered the family together to thank them for the celebration. He also shared that the bank seemed to have troubles and he was uneasy about the future. He suggested to Elizabeth and Eli that they should close their Trust Fund and take the cash. Eli agreed with Richard as he felt the same uneasiness. Eli, being an Assistant Editor of the Somerset Courier, could sniff a story from a mile away. "What is it, Richard? Something else I think."

"Well, I've been furloughed from the bank." He hung his head. "I anticipate that I will, like twenty other men in my department, lose my job at the end of the month." "However, I am more fortunate than most in my office. I have a productive farm and we will not starve."

The family sat in silence, "Are you certain?" Sachi asked.

Richard reached out and took her hand. Sachi was always at his right side by the dinner table. "I am fairly certain," he said. "East River National is about to be bought by a larger bank. I can't see how they can accommodate everyone."

"Very well." Alan said. "What I can do now is make plans to sustain this family. First crops to us, then we'll see what we can sell."

Richard smiled. "Good practical Alan. I am glad you are stepping up to the plate to help mom and me run the farm." He looked at Sachi. "Isn't it a good thing, Sachi?"

August 14, 1929

The crash of the stock market!

Thank goodness Eli and Elizabeth had taken Richard's advice to close their Trust Funds and withdraw the remaining cash.

Days after the crash, Richard could see that his efficient farm was competing for hundreds of other overproducing farms. So much corn, wheat, and meat rotted away. All over the country farmers were rich one year and poor the next.

Richard let his family know their very dire situation. "As you know, we are in the midst of a terrible time," Richard sighed. "I had to let the farm foreman go and we'll have to rely on Alan to make a better accounting of the farm." "Alan will also need the help of the twins."

"I will do whatever is necessary," Alan said. He felt badly for the foreman, he was older and not much liked by his family, who agreed to take him in. "I will not disappoint you," he promised his dad.

Even though the situation on the Tilridge Farm was disheartening, Richard was still generous and he supplied small plots of land to those who had been unable to live in the town or find a job to support their family. In turn, the people would work his land. There was no electric, no running water and candles were at a premium. But as much as they worked the land and as abundant as the harvest was, there were very few markets and grain commissioners around to purchase the staggered yields.

Nothing on the farm was selling well—not because it wasn't worthy of purchase but because no one had cash any longer. Investment opportunities were dwindling. It was all Richard could do to keep both tractors running. Byron Lopher, his mechanic extraordinaire, had sold his shop in town. "I'm headed to the assembly line in Detroit," he confided to Richard. "The pay's good and I can do the work. I'd rather do that than hound all my friends about their overdue bills."

Richard shook hands with Lopher. "I'll miss you."

"Naw, William Bolbecker's your man," Lopher told him. "He's younger and smarter and he's got more energy than I'll ever have. Besides, he needs the cash. His wife is due any day now. Baby number five."

"You'll not be sorry to go?" asked Richard.

"No. I want to say good bye to my friends and take my Francie and Joe to a better place. There's nothing here for us anymore."

Lopher's sentiment was similar to most in the area who were moving away. Families move in, then months later, moved out. There was a mass migration from the cities and toward the open land. Broke and starving, many looked for work in areas west of the Delaware River. Some went farther, they went west of the Mississippi. So many farmers and tradesman had traded their trusty draft horses for tractors and other machinery. Now, they were selling the tractors for pennies.

1933

Living on a farm, meant contributing to the community of farmers. Times were hard, so Harry often helped other farmers bale hay, plow fields run a feed truck and milk cows. The country had sunk into an awful state during the depression but Harry still managed to play his accordion and be happy while he played. They were calling it the Great Depression. All Harry knew was that he had the good luck to fall in love with the daughter of the farmer who lived across the street from him. She was barely the slip of a girl. But his heart sang when he saw her. Little Mabel Mercer. Her family had the clothes on their backs, no running water and no electricity.

No different for most farms. Truth be told, most farms couldn't afford electricity anyway. This was the same for many farmers. Outhouses were still used, hand pumps in shallow wells provided water and kerosene lamps provided light. Most of the local banks had closed and the stock market woes plunged people into an even greater depression.

CHAPTER ELEVEN

*"In order to save American soldiers' lives, we must provide the
lumber our armed forces need--now!"*
--Robert P. Patterson, Under Secretary of War, 1940-45

Dan laughed. "Okay, I'll talk to Gilly and Ken. I'm sure
they could change their minds about this tree. Who doesn't
love a good ghost story?"

"Hey, it's almost All Hallows Eve," Pastor Tom said. "Why don't you stick around? You could see the mist too."

"Uh, no thanks. I'm only interested in the tree's records."

"Okay, anything in particular?"

"Yeah, anything you have about date for the tree's cabling, what tree companies were involved, and if they're still around. Oh, and whatever you got on that big rock of cement that's inside."

"Oh yeah, the cement. That's easily a hundred years ago," Pastor Tom mused. "Let's hit the museum."

"You have a museum?" Lillian was intrigued

"Not really, that's me, making a joke," Pastor Tom confessed. "Since we have so much information on the tree, we've outgrown and expanded the church office." He led Dan and Lillian to a small building next to the church. "This was the old rectory," he said and unlocked the door. "See? We've turned it into an office and our 'tree museum.'

Where we charge everybody a dollar and half to see 'em."

"Oh, there's a fee?" Lillian reached into her purse.

"No," sighed Pastor Tom. "That's me, making a joke again."

"You're not very good at the humor thing," Dan observed.

"Be quiet."

Dan winked at Lillian. Pastor Tom went straight to the file cabinet and the drawer that read 1920s-1940s. He pulled out a few files and spread them on the table.

Dan texted Gilly and Ken, *Stuff 2 c. GHN!*

Inside the files were old receipts, letters and invoices. Carefully preserved notes from Pastor Tom's predecessors, paper documents and letters with watermarks, a few pressed leaves sandwiched between waxed paper and old photos. He pulled out records and a slim journal that read "Cavity Repair—White Oak."

"Perfect, thanks." Dan pulled up a chair.

"What's this?" Lillian cried. "Oh gosh! It's the exact same one!" She held up a laminated post card. It was the same black and white card she discovered in her mother's purse. "Look!" She fished out her original and compared the two.

"Yes, they're exactly alike," Pastor Tom said, looking at her. "Is that a problem?"

"She was here!"

Dan explained to the confused pastor. "My mom found this postcard and we're trying to figure out how my grandmother got it."

"She never went anywhere," Lillian told Pastor Tom. "She never told anyone that she came here. She lived in Pine Grove all her life. They never even went on a family vacation to the shore."

"Well, it wasn't the eighth wonder of the world, but our Great White Oak Tree was a tourist attraction back in the day," Pastor Tom said. He sifted through some World War II era newspapers and showed her. "They were going to chop it down. For the war effort, you know. But the town begged the Lumber Association of New Jersey to go elsewhere. Since there were thousands of acres of pine—they left it alone. So, it was the 'saved tree' and the soldiers used to come here to visit. There used to be a spur—like a transit loop. The soldiers and navy seamen would hop on the spur to Gladstone—it took you by the Great Swamp—and you could stop here. It was only a ninety-minute trip from Grand Central Station or was that Newark? I don't remember."

Lillian began to cry.

"Mom," Dan said, alarmed. "Now what's going on?"

"I think they were here," she sniffled. "I think they were both here."

Gilly and Ken entered only to see Lillian crying. "Uh-oh, let's get out of here."

Pastor Tom handed Lillian a tissue. "No, no, don't mind me." Lillian dabbed at her eyes and waved the two men back into the room. "It's so sweet. And now it all makes sense."

Gilly looked at Dan.

Dan shrugged.

"What makes sense?"

"My grandparents," Dan began. "They might have been here under the Great Oak."

Lillian started to weep again.

1934

In the middle of the Great Depression, Harry and Mabel married. Harry was happy. The "thirsty thirties" as locals called them had been good to him and Mabel. They made their home with his parents since his father's health was failing and his mother needed help with the farm. Mother Mars was a great help to Mabel. Elizabeth taught Mabel many household skills, like quilting, knitting and canning along with money management. Mabel made a good home for all of them.

Harry worked the farm along with working in the coal mine. The days were long and tough, but business was coming back and he was able to save up enough money to buy a car.

By 1941 Harry and Mabel had four kids (Susan, Eddie, Dana and Karen) running around the back yard. Harry's parents had died and they were greatly missed. He'd read the paper in the evening, while Mabel was putting the kids to sleep with prayers and stories and a few lullabies. On weekends, he'd treat the kids to a number of wild polka waltzes on the accordion. On Sunday gatherings he'd do a few rounds of polkas that no one but he knew the words to. He'd serenade Mabel with a favorite of hers, *"My Only Sunshine"* which made her cry. She was getting so weepy lately and he couldn't figure it out.

"Something's coming," she said. "I'm not sure what, but it is coming." She had been listening to the radio, and the news was nothing but tensions and battles in Europe. So far away he thought. Too far away. She was brushing at her eyes one night while stacking the dishes in the cupboard.

"Hey now you," Harry hugged her. Put down the dishes, let's talk about your tears."

"I'm not crying," she lied.

"Look, Mabel, let's think this out," he said. "You're a reasonable person. If your neighbor the next farm over gets into a fight, is it your fight?"

"No," she sniffled.

"Exactly," he said still holding her. "It's like us with all those countries, it's not our fight let them handle it."

Mabel was firm. "I don't like this Hitler fella. I think he's going to make it everyone's fight."

"You're not the only one who thinks that," Harry said. "He's pretty fired up most of the time."

"What's he saying exactly?"

"Phew, what isn't he saying?" Harry groaned. "Seems he's got a bone to pick with a lot of people," Harry said. "He seems to be sure that Germany is in a good way. They're recovered and are ready to, I don't know, show some muscle?"

"Like how?"

"Mabel, I don't know, I only know that FDR isn't going to get us into a war. We just got out of the tank."

But Mabel wasn't comforted by Harry's take on European relations. The invasions sounded much like war. She wasn't able to keep the fear out of the pit of her stomach. The women she knew, were using words like drafts and training in faraway places called Achille, Georgia and El Segundo, California. She couldn't let go of Harry. He worked hard to keep them afloat. Only a few years back, he'd taken up with the local miner's union. Work was dirty, but it gave them a decent living and they never went cold in the winter. He couldn't go. For the first time in her life, she felt very young and helpless. And she hated it.

As the relations in Europe deteriorated, they became more newsworthy. Invasion of this or that country was all anyone could talk about. Mabel's dread increased daily. Men were starting to openly talk war and women were starting to talk coffee cans. Every mother and her daughter had mad money stashed in a coffee can tucked in the back of their cupboard.

David Schneck

War meant stashing pennies, because the rainy days were on their doorstep. Again.

Somehow the Mars family was able to ease through 1940. Stock market crashes and Dust Bowls felt like ancient history. The mines were producing coal, and a living for many Pine Grove residents. The farm was reliably feeding Harry's kids, with a great deal of work from Mabel. Children, cows and chickens—her three C's. There wasn't a day that went by where Harry didn't brag about his wife. He'd tell the men as he sat with them for lunch about her cooking, her kindness and her grit.

"But God help me, that woman cannot sing."

On January 1, 1941 Pine Grove experienced a bizarre thaw. As soon as the sun came up, the ice began to melt. The icicles on the gutters dripped, the roads became slushy and the New Year felt like spring. After three days of eerie warmth, the area plunged back into more seasonal freezing weather. The old women shrugged back into their shawls and warned everyone this is not good, not good at all. Superstitious nonsense, the younger people laughed.

The old women were mocked until December. A touch of warm weather returned after Thanksgiving that year. It was welcomed by all.

On December 7, 1941, the second Sunday of Advent for Christians, shocking news began to circulate. Penelope Lambert, the post mistress of Pine Grove, Mayor Fred O'Connell and Chief of Police, Sam Kimmel learned the same thing in three different ways. Penelope had the luxury of a phone and was chatting with her sister in San Francisco. She screamed and dropped the phone. Fred's brother who was in the Navy, relayed bizarre information via a telegram, UNDER ATTACK STOP TELL MOM NOT TO WORRY STOP. Sam had invested in a ham radio--better than the crackling old dispatch radio. He picked up a Chicago radio announcer yelling and crying. The news seared through him.

Pearl Harbor was an inferno. The entire island territory was being bombed. No one was immune to the shock. No warning, just a note saying that peace negotiations with Japan were at an end. War was declared.

"That's it," Harry told Mabel. "This country doesn't like getting sucker punched." Even the president said, "This day would live in infamy." He demanded a declaration of war.

Mabel knew that her neighbor's fight would now be hers. Harry was wrong and that Sunday evening, they gathered in the church and prayed. Almost immediately, life changed in Pine Grove.

After war was declared, patriotic men—boys, husband and grandfathers, enlisted. Not all who enlisted were accepted as soldier material. The men had to be healthy, young and between the ages of 21 and 35. Naturally, those already in the armed services were to be called up, regardless of age.

After numerous waves of propaganda, the military had a vast quantity of fighting troops. And after a few battles, the navy had numerous waves of casualties. Mayor O'Connell's brother was the first of Pine Grove residents to succumb to injuries sustained at the Pearl Harbor attack.

The year ground on. Gold Star mothers were growing exponentially. Black crepe draped over the church. Boys were streaming overseas and not returning. Rations, metal and rubber drives became the norm. A year slipped by, then another. By 1943 it seemed like something was going wrong. The Germans weren't as dumb as they were portrayed and the Japanese showed no signs of slowing down. Why hadn't the war been over and won? Why weren't the men coming home victorious? Someone had made a huge miscalculation. Mabel's stomach wasn't accepting much food these days.

Reesa Tarden and her sister, Nina had gone to work in the steel mills in Harrisburg. Their parents had died long ago and their brother was killed at Savo Island in the Pacific on August 8, 1942. There was nothing for them here. Neither woman was keen on any fellas—those that were left in Pine Grove were married or grandfathers. Mabel wasn't breathing easier as the world was almost through with 1943.

1944

Harry received a yellow letter with "Order to Report for Induction" on All Saints Day. He was to report to Ft. Benning, Georgia, on January 22 for basic training.

Mabel was beside herself. "How can they draft you? You're over thirty, and a sole provider! You have a family— me, the kids. How can they do this? You have to ask for an exemption."

Harry pointed to the *Willful Failure to Report Promptly to This Board* section of the document. "I have to go."

Mabel fumed.

Harry wasn't exactly panicked about it. Nor was he talking like the boys in town who thought it was going to be an adventure. They were actually chomping at the bit to go and see the world. It had been nearly 30 years since the last engagement and some of the older grandpas were shaking their heads. You won't see the world. What you will see will change you forever and not in a good way.

He packed an old concertina lent to him by Mr. Verggio, the grocer. He told Harry, "Play when you get lonely, itta make you happy *molto veloce*." And there was no way he was going to haul old Bess his accordion halfway around the world. He said good-bye to the kids hugged them, kissed them, told them to mind their mother and be good to their aunts. When he came to say good bye to Mabel, she was nowhere to be found. He walked into the barn again. He could hear her rustling around behind the cow.

Harry made sure his '37 Chevy was blocked up off the wheels. Since Mabel didn't drive, it was going to just sit. Putting it up on blocks would save the tires from dry rot. He hoped she wouldn't donate them. Since the end of '41, there was a ban on the sale of new tires. For the cause, they were told.

"I'm leaving, Mabel," he yelled into the barn.

Mabel stood up. Her brown eyes were shining with tears, her mouth in a tight line. "Don't go." It was all she said. Then she sat down and went back to milk the cow.

Unwilling to make a scene, he left.

At boot camp, Harry was teased by the younger men. A few attempted to call him "grandpa," but since there were many men, officers and drill sergeants older than Harry, the nickname never stuck. Instead, they called him Squeeze Box. In the moments of quiet before lights out when the men were chatting, Harry would pull out the concertina, and play polkas. They sounded haunting and lonely because he was never able to get the bellows right.

Weeks turned into months and in March, they were finished with boot camp. Harry, trained as a gunner, was less uneasy about his orders overseas than he was with the dullness in his heart. He had to see Mabel before he left. Harry was not a believer in letting things go. He hated unfinished business. He had some things to say to Mabel. He was sure she had something to say to him.

Dear Mabel,

I had to write. I found out that my orders to ship out got thrashed. I'll only get 12 hours of leave before I ship out. We're taking the transport up to New York City harbor and shoving off from there. Rumor has it, we'll be on the Queen Mary.

I miss you. We never made a proper goodbye. Don't be angry. I had to go. But I have a plan. We leave on Thursday, it's a whole day on the train, but there's a stop at Newark. According to the transport map, there's a Gladstone East spur. I can get to

Basking Ridge, New Jersey. Remember Basking Ridge is where my family roots are and I can't believe I'll get to see the town again. I visited the Tilridge Farm when I was 14 years old. My Uncle Alan was taking me to New York City and we stopped at the farm on our way to the city. It was the last time I saw Grandpa Richard and grandma Sachi. Please meet me there.

One of the guys (Frank Delaney) from boot camp is from there. I'm riding with him. I guess they're afraid we'll desert if we don't stick tight. Ha-ha. By the time you get this letter, it will be time to get on the bus. Remember, Basking Ridge, New Jersey. There's a Great Oak Tree by the church. I know how much you like trees and you will want to see this one.

Love always,

Harry

Mabel counted her pennies, told Emily to watch the kids, bought a ticket and took the eastbound New Jersey Greyhound bus. What an awful bumpy drive. She gulped and burped a hundred times. Not more denial; she had to be pregnant.

The bus rumbled into town and the beautiful white church caught her eye. But leaning against the post office was Harry, leaning just as careless as you please. Oh, what a sight for her eyes.

"Harry! Harry!"

"Well, there you are! What took you so long?" He trotted towards her.

"I would have been here sooner, but I, uh I," she stammered. *Should I tell him that I'm pregnant?* "Well, the bus driver stopped a few times. He told everyone it would take just under three hours."

"Ah, what does he know?" Harry dismissed the driver's knowledge of maps and distance calculation. "Come here," he said and scooped her up. He hugged her so hard she squealed.

"Put me down!"

"Honey I got four hours left," he whispered in her ear. "I'm not letting go."

"Harry, I'm sorry I was so mad. But it's wrong. The country is going to run out of men--out of sons and fathers and husbands. I can't run out of you. I wish you'd stay."

He smiled. "I can't. I'm all trained up, I can crawl on my belly in the mud and shoot an M3. I may lose my hearing but it's for a good cause, right?"

"Don't joke, I need to tell you something," she fought to keep the tears out of her voice.

"What?"

"Come back."

He gripped her hand. "Come on, let's walk." Down the sidewalk they went. They walked the streets pretending to be a normal couple during the war.

At the end of the road, they saw the church and the Great Oak Tree. "Let's say a prayer," Mabel begged. The massive oak tree hovered over grave stones. Spring hadn't visited its leaves, but the branches bobbed with hope for warmth.

"What?" he questioned. "A prayer in the church? Okay, alright."

The interior of the church was silent, stuffy and nearly airless. The perfect place to pray. After they were finished, Harry pulled Mabel outside. They stood under the tree's outstretched branches.

"Harry, you're coming home," Mabel said. "I just know it. You're not going to die."

"Listen to me Mabel, if anything happens," Harry began. "You need to get on with your life, okay?"

"No, shush don't talk like that," she said. "It makes me think you'll—" she stopped. "Well, I just can't think like that."

"Well, you're going to have to."

"Harry, I'm, I'm pregnant," Mabel stammered. "I can't do this without you."

Harry whistled. "Woo-wee, baby number five."

"Please be serious, this is serious."

Harry took her hands. "I know, I know. But you need to hear it from me, that it's okay. It's okay to move on."

Mabel shook her head. "You're coming home." It felt like she was telling God what to do. Harry was just too stubborn. Someone had to intervene.

He hugged her. "Gotta go sweetheart. My ride's gonna be here." He released her. They walked back to the post office and they went inside and bought a postcard. Mabel kissed the postcard and then placed it in her purse. They went outside and they had just enough time for last minute hugs and kisses. Harry kissed Mabel and kissed her until she was breathless. A small car arrived and collected the men in uniform and drove away leaving Mabel alone and already missing Harry.

Mabel walked back to the church and went to the Great Oak Tree which seemed to comfort her. She looked at the graves and prayed again for Harry's safety. When Mabel opened her eyes, she spied the name Tilridge on some of the Head Stones near the tree. She walked closer to the stones and could read Sarah Tilridge and Martha Tilridge on two of the stones but the third one just had TILLRID. It was time to catch the bus back to Pine Grove, back to her children and back to the farm. During her ride home, Mabel thought about the Tilridge family. "What did my mother-in-law tell me about the Tilridge family?" she asked herself. Mother Elizabeth would say that Harry's father Axel was a true Tilridge but Grandpa Richard just shared the Tilridge name, they were connected but not connected. Mother Elizabeth talked about the Johnstown flood and how Richard and Sachi raised her and her brother Eli. Her parents died in the flood and her maiden was Rink. The last time Harry and Mabel saw Uncle Eli was at Elizabeth's funeral. They lost track of Uncle Eli and Uncle Alan being busy with the farm and the children. "I wonder if they are still living, how old would they be now, and do they know why Uncle Alan is and isn't Harry's uncle?" Mabel

pondered while the bus bumped towards Pine Grove. Mabel dozed and dreamed of the Great Oak Tree, it was singing to her
----

I was here before you.
I will be here with you.
I will live here after you.

Harry sailed out New York Harbor on the finest luxury vessel on the planet. But with over 10,000 men, which was over three times the limit, The Queen Mary was stripped down to her skivvies. "Sardines have more room," someone complained. The ship was headed to Europe and this voyage was to port in Scotland. The Army had to use several ports-of-call with so many men arriving so quickly. Two weeks on the ocean was horrible. A lot of men got seasick as the boat tossed and rolled. To keep from getting seasick, Harry filled his mind with memories of Mabel and there last hours together. He thought about the Basking Ridge postcard they bought at the Post Office. He told her, "If I don't come home, rip it up and go on without me." She kissed the postcard, put it in her purse, looked at him and said, "You are coming home to me." Then he kissed her and kissed her until she was breathless.

Once they landed in Scotland, the men were organized into units for special training in preparation for D-Day invasion. Harry and his unit went to Belfast, Ireland for their special training. They trained for four months. In early July, the Army of Patton's 5th infantry division, 10th Regiment with Harry Mars, anti-tank gunner was ordered to head to Europe and go take out Panzers and Tigers. Their goal was to land on Utah

Beach, Normandy, France, a month after D-Day and push east to the border town of Metz.

Their mood was all nervous energy. "Hey Harry, we gonna see fireworks for 4th of July?"

"Just follow my rockets' red glare."

The first day on French soil, the soldiers began their work in earnest. The whole countryside was full of rain and mud. The night was cold and muddy. The next day was muddy. They ate and slept in mud. Once the area was secured, they headed to Metz and remained pinned down for weeks.

Harry woke up in his coat shivering. More rain, more mud. Supplies were low. Did Patton even know they were here?

"Wake up girls!" the captain yelled. "Time for some clean up."

"Dammit we're soldiers, not janitors," grumbled one of the men.

The brigade marched a mile south to the remains of Le fleurs des Germaine.

"Take a look, boys," the captain said. "They're bulldozing it tomorrow."

Harry was saddened at the idea of a whole village—a place where people had been born, lived, got married, had kids and tried to fight off the Nazis—was going to be wiped out to make a road for tanks. "Aw, don't get sentimental about it, Mars," one of the men in his unit chided. "It ain't like anybody cares. Looks like this place was abandoned years ago." It was true. Several structures that resembled homes, were crumbling, the main road was littered with broken carts and other unusable farm equipment. No glass in the windows, no sign of life. A *ville oubliée.* Still, Harry gave the town a good look and tried to memorize the nooks and crannies. This town could have been Pine Grove, just as remote and as easily forgotten. There was some yelling at the front of the line. The words were being passed down soldier to soldier. New orders. The 10th regiment was to continue east but then south to the mountainous Ardennes region.

CHAPTER TWELVE

"He who plants a tree, plants a hope."
--Lucy Larcom, Wheaton Female Seminary, 1860

"So, exactly what makes sense?" Pastor Tom asked, handing Lillian another tissue.

"No, no, don't mind me." Lillian dabbed at her eyes. "It's so sweet. And now it all makes sense."

"I think what my mom is trying to say, is that we've come full circle," Dan explained. "Mom knows her mother was here."

"We just think this was where she said goodbye to Dad, their last day together before Dad shipped out to fight in the war," explained Dan

"Dan and Pastor Tom, I also feel that there is something else, there's a feeling about the Great Oak Tree and its roots that haunts me," Lillian added.

Fall 1944

Mabel cradled her fifth baby. A lively little girl who squirmed more than she cried. Her name didn't come immediately. Mabel and Harry were the kind of parents who didn't pick out names prior to the baby's arrival. Certainly, they'd remember ancestor and family names. But with so many cousins with similar names there wasn't much leftover to honor a loved one's memory.

Mabel looked at the few cards and flowers on her kitchen table. Her first child's gifts filled up the house with food and flowers and cards stuffed with cash. October made it difficult to get flowers so there was more food this time. A pot of homegrown mums sat next to her kitchen sink. Poor man's lilies her mother used to call them. They looked nothing like lilies, it was just a mother's dream of flowers in her home. A mum's brightness and cheery color always made fall's chill bearable.

Lilly, Lillian. She wrote it down for the birth certificate forms and wrote it carefully in the family Bible.

Mabel was questioned, no absolutely grilled by her relatives.

"Why not Sookie? I like that name," one of her cousins suggested.

"Why not Alice?" asked another. "Great Aunt Alice should be remembered."

Mabel shook her head. "No, Lillian or Lily, that's what the baby's name will be."

Fall 1944

His unit's motto of, "we will" was changed to "we would if we had food." Captain Rice, tired of walking in line like a "damned funeral procession without the hearse," took a back road not on any map. The intent was to circumvent the waiting line. The commanders were alerted that the tail end of the 3rd army needed several hours just to cross the bridge at *La Haye du Puits.*

Harry had sat in a bomb crater along with three other half-frozen men for half a day. The major hold-up was that the 28th infantry had to get jeeps and thirteen tanks across a narrow bridge intersection north of Reims. Captain Rice was told that the main roadways had been shelled deliberately by the retreating Germans. There were no roads and the bridges were demolished.

And now, since there was no other place for the unit to bed down, they had to eat and sleep where they were stalled. After the most miserable day of his life, starving, thirsty and no latrine shovel, Captain Rice gave the order to move— somewhere—just move. A messenger from the Occupational Specialties interrupted their progress. "Oh, for the love of Mike!" yelled Captain Rice.

"What's up, Cap?" Harry asked.

"New orders," Captain Rice snapped. "We're to advance southeast, now."

One of the men in the unit scratched his head "What gives? We just got orders last week to go northwest."

Harry shook his head. "Just move along soldier," he joked, pushing the man forward. "I hear there's a good diner up ahead."

The unit did encounter other brigades. Nearly all were either wounded or on orders to return to 3rd army HQ which had moved from Le Mans to Paris.

Harry's unit met up with a pilot from the airborne division that was also heading back to Paris. He had been injured when he crashed his plane, heavily damaged by German panzers' artillery. Lucky fellow. He had only broken his leg and his arm. Some fellows were missing both legs. Harry was told by the pilot that the French people treated him very well. The pilot told him that this was how it was all over France. Thankfully French farmers generously traded fresh eggs for a GI's supply of candy and cigarettes. He said they were so kind; the farm wives would wash their uniforms. "Do you know what it's like to have a clean fresh uniform?"

"No," said Harry. "I can't remember what it is like to have a clean, fresh anything."

The pilot was quiet for a moment. "Well Harry, I hope you get some of that French wine, maybe even that cognac before this is all over."

"Naw, I doubt that'll happen."

"Have hope fella, maybe something good will happen."

The good thing that happened was that Harry was utilized to interrogate German soldiers. The purpose was to gain any information about the size and location of the enemy.

"Look, Mars," Captain Rice began. "Anyone who can speak fluent anything needs to help out." He looked Harry in the eye. "You're a gunner, not intelligence, so you can opt out, you know."

Harry hesitated. Then thought, maybe if I do this I can get out of here quicker. "Tell me where you want me."

Harry was requested to report to the front of the line. He was instructed to accompany a soldier from the 2nd division. Escorted to an interrogation area, he was flanked by special ops officers who begged Harry to ask a few questions—location of the *Militärverwaltung* in Frankreich. Seems the conflicting information of the German Administration which was supposed to have disbanded after Paris was freed, was costing lives. Every time one piece of intelligence proclaimed the village to be German-free, some poor private got their brains blown out by a sniper. They'd lose a village, gain a hill but nothing decisive and it was making the Allies look bad.

"None of this is official," said Officer Bob Young. "Our interpreter got dysentery and we need someone to talk to these guys before we transfer them." He pointed to a muddy section of road. "We caught these guys in a field south of here," Young said. "We're not sure if there are more."

On the ground, sitting crossed legged were three German prisoners. Two were younger, 20s maybe and the last was about Harry's age. Geeze, thought Harry, they look as bad as we do. And they smell worse. He wondered if all soldiers were treated universally rotten by their commanding officers and generals. And gypped out of food and decent boots.

Young's buddy was Officer Tom Jenkins. "We cornered them in a barn," he said nudging Harry. "That explains their lovely aroma," he joked. "They're not talking and so help me, I'm in a mood to slap them back to Berlin. See what you can get out of them. We want to find out if they know anything about counter offensives."

Harry nodded and took a few cigarettes from his breast pocket. He lit four of them and handed one to each of the soldiers. He kept the last for himself.

"*Gehen Sie vor, nehmen Sie eine*" Harry urged the soldiers.

They looked shocked at the generous offer and accepted the cigarettes. Each soldier expressed their gratitude, with a *danke*. Harry noted that Rotten krauts though they were, they still were polite. Germans back home were always stereotyped as rude and stupid. The exact opposite was on display.

Harry asked them in respectful tones how they were feeling and when was the last time they had eaten a decent meal. He ignored the obvious what's your name? And, how are you? The younger soldiers were more forthcoming, answering in more than one or two word explanations. He chatted a little bit with them, told them he had a cousin in Stuttgart. He discovered where they were from—small towns in southeastern Germany. He asked if they had ever been to Munich where the beer so was delicious you wouldn't want to drink anywhere else. As he hoped, the prisoners let their guard down. They smiled and nodded.

Harry asked for a map and knelt beside the German prisoners. He pointed to Reims, *"Woche hier waren?"* he asked. One of them nodded, "ja" He began tracing a line toward Luxembourg.

The oldest grabbed at the map. *"Nien! Sagen Sie ihm nichts!"*

Harry's fellow GIs shoved the older German back into his sitting position.

"It's okay," Harry said, pulling Young and Jenkins back into place behind him. "No need for the rough stuff." He turned and winked at them. "Yet." They chuckled. He hid his body and placed a star next to a German border town on the map and handed it back. "Thanks, just hold on to that, will ya?"

The older German, still younger than Harry, understood that it was not appropriate to let the enemy know the path they were headed. The younger men, probably yearning for a decent bath and a meal, hadn't been soldiers long enough to know the rules of engagement. Or what to say if you're taken prisoner. Even after the enemy shows some common human decency. That is, no matter what, no soldier gave anything other than name, rank and serial number.

Harry inhaled deeply. He spoke to the older German and inquired if he was surprised that he was captured. The older German shrugged. Harry asked if he was surprised that he had not been killed. The German paused but still shrugged. Harry then asked if he was also surprised that the Allies met Hitler in Saarbrücken. The German's alarm gave him away.

"Nein, das ist nicht möglich!"

This time it was Harry's turn to shrug. *"Ja, ist möglich."*

The man hung his head. His forehead wrinkled in thought. Harry could see that he was puzzled. The implausible had happened.

The German looked up defiant. *"Dass du ein Lügner bist."*

Harry smiled. *"Nein, ich bin kein Lügner."* He showed the German the map again and pointed to the starred city. *"Siehst du das?"*

Harry explained that red stars always indicated enemy defeat on Allies' maps. The older German slowly accepted the lie.

Harry pushed the map in the man's face. *"es ist vorbei."* The other German prisoners looked positively sick. Hitler's defeat would end everything for them. The war, their lives and any chance of returning home.

Harry asked a few more questions of them, but they were now stone faced and silent.

"I'm done," Harry said. "Can I talk to your CO?"

Young and Jenkins hustled Harry through the series of tents and jeeps. Harry informed their CO that the path the Germans were taking, looked like a retreat but was in fact a doubling up of an offensive. The German army was returning to meet Hitler for an enormous counter strike. The CO nodded. It made sense. Hitler may have lost France, but he would not lose Germany. Harry also knew it meant the 1st and 3rd army were racing across France to confront the monster on his own territory. Harry was thanked, given an extra carton of cigarettes and a case of baked beans for his interrogation work.

"Don't go anywhere Mars," the CO said. "We may need you again."

"I'll be here," Harry said. "Got nothing else to do."

He returned to his unit and a day later they heaved out of their encampment, such as it was and moved on. Captain Rice said they were bound for Metz. It was going to be an easy go of it, they were promised. The summer dragged on with hot days and cool damp nights. Boots were wearing out along with the men's tempers. By the time they arrived in Metz near the end of September, the only safe place was smoldering trenches created by the German army's artillery. Captain Rice ordered the men to take cover in the blackened earth bunkers.

By the end of September, Harry had a fairly good idea that they weren't going anywhere. September crept into October and October into November. Every time they rallied forward; they were easily repulsed by the enemy.

Some creative and bored soul carved a Jack-o-Lantern face in a 152 mm dud. Halloween already, Harry thought. My God, the baby had to have been born by now. He wondered what the baby's name would be. He hoped if the baby was a girl, she wasn't going to give Mabel too much trouble. And if it was a boy, he hoped it wouldn't be too loud. She should probably have a pretty name. Something feminine and girly.

It was cold for October. Bitter winds and steady drizzle made some of the guns freeze in their hostler. Some men without decent gloves were losing finger tips to frostbite. If this is October, thought Harry, what will winter be like?

It wasn't as though Patton's army wasn't trying. They were fighting hard and dying. But they weren't dying in battle they were dying because the army was so poorly supplied. There was a rumor that HQ received blankets and were enjoying them, while the 10th regiment received shell casings and climbing rope.

"What are we supposed to do, Cap?" asked one private. "Hang ourselves?"

"Dammit," Captain Frank Rice cursed. "I begged for ammunition a month ago! What the hell are we supposed to do now, throw them at the Krauts?" He got on a radio and screamed for a good five minutes. The voice on the other end only answered with a "yes sir, thank you sir."

Harry didn't blame Captain Rice. The officer knew the men needed food, boots and blankets. Some of the men couldn't even hold a weapon properly, their hands shook so much. Not from fear, but from hunger and cold.

So, this was Patton's brilliant 3rd Army? Men without food, frozen fingers and toes, no boots, no coats and even no ammunition. Harry was in the 5th infantry division 10th regiment. He knew there were at least three dozen other divisions--infantry, armor and airborne--plowing across France. He knew that sooner or later they'd slam into Germans. All he had to do was look around. When they had hit the shore of Normandy bodies were still washing up on shore. They'd marched past a German soldier. His body left in the middle of the road, run over so many times his torso was separated from his legs. Nothing seemed real any more.

Harry was jealous of the other men who wrote home, once if not twice a week. Their voluminous scribbling, made him feel stupid. He envied them for having the ability of coming up with page after page of things to say. Here he was able to speak three languages fluently, even understand some Dutch, but barely able to grab a postcard and write his name and the date.

What could he say? He was freezing. He longed for Mabel's chicken soup. That he desperately wanted to hold his newborn baby--boy? Girl? How could he tell Mabel he had been having nightmares about parts of men littering his farm field? He was unable to sleep because he agonized about a little baby who may never see its father. He wanted to punch Patton in the face. Why was it that soldiers did all of the dirty, hard work and got none of the credit? Why couldn't he write like Uncle Eli?

The men lost track of the days, until one of them said. "Well, what the hell, it's Thanksgiving." There was a slight edge that Harry noticed, a slight pulling back by the enemy. They crept out of their holes and crawled along toward the border. Only 77 kilometers to Saarbrücken. Harry hoped that by the time they'd get to Germany, the Nazis would surrender. But no dice even through the 3rd Army was successful in the battle of Metz (the Lorraine Campaign) which ended December 13.

Winter exploded in full. Christmas 1944, it should have been a grand day with the kids hopping all over the place up at the crack of dawn. Not letting him and Mabel sleep a wink. She insisted on hiding their presents in the same places so the kids practically knew what they were getting weeks before the big day. Instead, Harry woke up to a dead man. Private Brant Witherspoon of Cambridge, Massachusetts had died over night. Most likely died of hypothermia along with the injuries he sustained at *Havre de Campeign* where they met up with a small band of isolated German gunners.

That Wednesday after Christmas, Captain Rice handed out new boots and winter gear. Even though the situation was stalemated, it felt like a rest to Harry. After 12 days of shooting until his ears rang, the struggle got worse.

Captain Rice, already wounded begged for the retreat to collect with the 11th and then re-engage the enemy. The upper level of command wouldn't hear of it. The fighting only got more brutal. They were unable to drive each other back.

"All we're doing is emptying our guns," one soldier complained. "Were not getting anywhere."

The New Year brought new hope. The Germans thrust themselves at the Allies line in a risky, last ditch effort. But the very thing that protected them ended up being the very thing that defeated them. The Ardennes was a forest without equal. Trees so thick and lush it was easy to hide but impossible to get their tanks through. Unable to sustain the heavy casualties or gain any ground without artillery support, the Germans back tracked and gave the Allies a huge victory in the Battle of the Bulge on January 25, 1945.

February didn't thaw the brutal winter. The world would just not get warmer. In the beginning of March, a week from Harry's birthday, the ground was still frozen solid. His regiment had been dragging themselves from one cold mud puddle to the next. Too cold to sleep outside but too wet to light a fire and get warm plus, they were warned about light fires—they were dead giveaways for the enemy.

They continued to march through mud and ice. Harry once again was called to the front line for interrogation, but by time he arrived, the battle-weary sergeant shot the German.

Harry woke up the day of his birthday from a beautiful dream. He was at the Great Oak Tree in New Jersey holding Mabel in his arms. He was saying goodbye and she was telling him he wasn't going to die. It was warm. And he heard a woodpecker and he heard the Great Oak Tree singing which comforted him.

"Get down! Get down!"

Mud puddles exploded everywhere. Some sharpshooter nearby found extra ammunition, thought Harry. Enough of that crap. He grabbed his rifle and fired back. Time to take a breather, he thought. I am getting too old for this.

"Cease fire!" The command couldn't have come sooner. Harry was relieved.

"Save your ammo!"

The 5th Infantry Division arrived at Oppenheim under heavy fire from Germans they couldn't see. They had to get across the river but it was impossible to do during the daylight hours. Captain Rice told the men they'd be crossing the Rhine River at night to avoid being picked off like fish in barrel. So on the night of March 22 they crossed the Rhine without the usual artillery preparations and surprised the Germans. The 3rd Army was involved in four river assaults with the first being at Oppenheim followed by Boppard, St. Goar and south of the city Mainz.

CHAPTER THIRTEEN

"A man doesn't plant a tree for himself.
He plants it for posterity."
– Alexander Smith, Scottish poet, 1861

They decided to grab a late lunch at The Blue Bird. Pastor Tom had a phone call from a congregant that needed his undivided attention. Ken and Gilly were wrapping up at the tree. The silence in the car made Dan nervous.

"Come on Mom, what's going on?"

"Nothing."

"Uh, no, there's definitely something," Dan argued. "You're too quiet."

"Look, I respect everything you've gone through so far. But I don't think you should take down that tree."

"Technically I'm not the one with the saw," Dan pointed out. "So, I'm not going to be—"

"Oh, you know what I mean," Lillian snapped. "Don't play games. "You know you're going to be a part of it."

"Yeah, I am and I think it's the best thing for everyone," Dan said. "For the tree's sake and for the general public's sake."

"I don't know."

"Mom, the tree is dead," Dan said. "And it was probably dying a hundred years ago. It's not growing anymore and it just isn't safe as it is now."

"Can't you just prune it a little?"

"No," Dan was firm. "Listen Mom, Pastor Tom isn't a dummy," Dan said. "If he has a choice between his flock and an old hazardous tree, he's going to pick people every time."

Lillian sighed. "How can I make you understand how much that tree means to me now?

"Mom I get it, it's nostalgic."

"No!" Lillian burst out. "It's more than that. My DNA is there on the tree. Mom was pregnant with me when she and Dad met there. So, I was there. I know my parents too. They said some really important things to each other before he went off to war. There's more to it than just nostalgia. I have a postcard for nostalgia. I need for that tree to live. And I think our ancestors are buried under it"

"What? Do you have proof?"

"Almost, I have been doing some research on the family name Tilridge and I just need to make one or two connections."

"Yes, Adam told me that you were at the Schuylkill County Courthouse searching marriage certificates and property deeds."

"It's kind of dead though."

"Stop being a smart ass, will you please?"

"Mom, calm down. I think I have a way of helping you keep that tree."

"You do? You're joking."

"Nope. I'm serious. I think I have a way to make that tree last, well, almost forever."

"Oh, my goodness. How? Tell me now," Lillian insisted.

"I will, but you have to buy me lunch first."

April 1945

After crossing the Rhine, the 3rd Army moved east into central and southern Germany. Fighting seemed to be less intense to Harry. Then out the blue his unit was under fire.

"Get Down! Get Down!" yelled the Captain.

Pain seared through Harry's gut.

He tried to stretch out but his body refused to let him straighten out.

"How you doing Mars?"

Harry tried to stand up. "I think I'm..." he paused and the world went black.

Waldkirchen, Germany

Harry woke up with clenched teeth. The pain in his gut was driving him insane. It seemed to come in cycles. Every fifteen minutes or so it hit him hard. And then it was five minutes of teeth-gritting, harsh-grunting and then he'd be good to go. Until the next 15 minutes came. The faces over him were blurred. Some sounded male, some sounded female. They were talking about him.

"How many, doctor?"

"One Syrette this time, wait 'til the quarter hour though. Too close together and we'll kill him."

Harry felt a cool hand on his forehead. He was oozing sweat and blood and pus and burning up with fever. That hand felt so good. Don't take it away, he thought.

"He's not doing well here," the female voice said. "We may need to move him again."

"Obviously we're sending him home," the male voice said. The voice sounded flustered.

"I didn't mean to upset you. I only think he's in need of something more ... intricate."

"I know."

"Is there anything we can—?"

"I'll contact the USS Relief," the male voice said. "Pack his bags I'll see if we can get him out of here by tomorrow."

"Yes, doctor."

The cool hand left his forehead and the pain returned with a vengeance.

"Doctor, he's ..."

"Give him the morphine."

"But you said ..."

"Give it to him now!"

Harry floated up off the gurney and then blacked out.

The days melted into one and then two and then after a week, Harry felt dizzy. His whole world was rocking. It wasn't a dizziness in his head, it was his whole body. What kind of meds were they giving me? This was too much. He tried to get out of bed. He needed to talk to someone in charge because nothing was making sense. He tried to stand up, a wave of nausea rolled over him. Like seasickness.

He was at sea.

In a coherent moment, Harry reached out a hand toward the attending physician who was close to his cot. "Hey, fella, where am I?" His throat felt like sandpaper.

"You're at sea, soldier," the doctor said. He was a young man, younger than Harry. But he had a good face and a good smile. Reassuring, not sappy. To Harry, he looked like a guy who would tell you the truth whether you liked it or not. "You're on the Larkspur. And you're heading home. Probably be there in about five or six days, depending on the weather. Do you have any folks in South Carolina?"

"No, why?"

"Because it's our first port of call."

***

Mabel took up knitting. Lots of women were making hats and scarves for the soldiers. "It's the least we can do, there are so many guys freezing from the frigid cold weather over there," said Mitzie Rogan. "They don't get care packages over in France." Mitzie's brother wrote regularly to her and her mother. Mabel was jealous of the all the news Mitzie was getting. But Mabel knew Harry. He was no letter writer.

"My Joey says that no one has the right kind of hats," Kathleen Switzer said. "He wrote me a letter saying that some guys don't even have boots." Kathleen's son also wrote home. Rumor had it he wasn't coming home, having fallen in love with a French mademoiselle. He wanted to stay there.

Mabel laughed. "It's not very good." She held up the gray knitted wool cap. "I betcha this wool hat goes to the soldiers in Guadalcanal." Knitting was yet another way to keep her hands busy and it was the least she could do. So many women had gone to work in the cities because manpower and men were in such short supply. Judging by the loss of life from the war, Mabel figured the women would have to stay in those jobs.

Sometimes a postcard would come in from Harry and she'd see a picture of a landmark in France. The Eiffel Tower looked pretty impressive. How amazing you got to see it in person, Harry, thought Mabel. Harry would only write his name and the date on the card. The postcards arrived about three months after the date. Mabel knew getting any kind of mail was a small miracle. The postcard that came that day which her son handed to her made her drop her yarn. The fluffy ball rolled off her lap and bounced across the floor, over to the baby's playpen.

Mabel read the postcard again--

Got sick. Coming home on a hospital ship. Will see you soon. Love Harry

The post card was dated, October 6, Charleston, SC. Mabel looked at the Pine Grove National Bank calendar, it was October 13. She left the knitting on the floor. She climbed up on a chair and got the coffee can down from the cabinet. Ripping the lid open she heard the coins ring all over the floor. She gathered them up and ran out of the house. She rounded up the kids and begged her oldest to watch Lillian for a few minutes. Mabel ran down the road and asked for a ride to the telegraph office in Hunters Run. She needed to get word out to everyone. Harry was home!

Harry was home. On American soil. Banged up a bit, but still here. In one piece. Mabel nearly fainted from relief. She didn't want a gold star on her window. She wanted a husband. She remembered their meeting under the oak tree. She had kept the postcard of the Great Oak in her purse tucked in her top drawer. She pulled it out every now and then at night when the kids were in bed. Sometimes it made her feel closer to Harry. Other times it felt like a lifetime again or someone else's life, entirely. Most of all she remembered it was the day that she told God what to do. Well, it seemed that God was very good at listening.

Harry stayed in South Carolina for what seemed like only minutes. He awoke to hear he was going to undergo surgery. But not here. They moved him, roughly, onto an ambulance transport to a train. He was transported on an old freight train that rocked as much as the ship did. In and out of consciousness, Harry was grateful for the morphine that seemed to make the intermittent pain bearable. It never went away. He felt like his teeth would break sometimes.

He arrived in upstate New York and was transported to Brentwood Military hospital.

"We'll take good care of you soldier," the attendant promised.

"Hope so," said Harry.

"Looks like you're slated for emergency surgery tomorrow," he frowned. "For an appendectomy. As well as exploratory for shrapnel in the gut."

"Just don't take out any good parts," Harry joked and then he passed out.

Once more Harry was on a train this time he was heading south. All he was told now was that the surgery went well, but he needed to be moved to a facility that specialized in rehabilitation. He was being sent to Valley Forge Hospital for final recuperation. The leaves in Pennsylvania were beautiful. He wrote to Mabel and told her he was getting closer and closer to home. The good news was that he was pretty sure they were done with his gut. The pain was gone but he had been on his back for so long, he needed to be taught how to walk again.

Those were the hardest days for him. Mabel wanted to visit. She'd ask her brother Tom to drive her to see him. But Harry said no. It killed him to say it. But he had to be stronger. His first step out of bed and he fell flat on his face. He wouldn't be humiliated like that in front of his wife. He grunted and groaned through two hours of walking "lessons" with crutches and then hopping around without them. He then was winded for almost the same amount of time. He felt exhausted. It also seemed to him, that he had to use the crapper for an abnormal length of time. Sometimes there was blood in the pot but other days it was all normal. Somewhere between Germany and the United States, Harry lost a bit of himself.

When he finally saw Mabel, he had a little ray of hope maybe things would be okay. She kissed him all over and asked a million questions, none of which she waited for the answer to. Tom helped him into the back of his car and took him home. Mabel waited on Harry hand and foot. Until one day he told her enough, he was going back to work.

He was not the same man. Harry worked harder than he ever did before. But he rarely enjoyed life. His concertina, miraculously spared harm during the war, was collecting dust in the attic. He acknowledged a few people but he had lost his sense of humor and maybe his sense of who he was.

While never cruel to his children, he found it hard to look at them. Small version of himself that he couldn't quite remember. Almost ignored them. He barely spoke. Only orders now and then. Take out the trash, help your mother. Gas up the tractor. The children sensed the difference and the mood in the house shifted from one of jubilation to somber silence.

One night, Mabel pulled him aside.

"Harry, Harry, we...we gotta talk," she stuttered. "You can't be a stone for the rest of your life."

Harry was quiet for a long while.

"Mabel, I want to talk but I just can't," he said finally. "Some of it's too horrible. I wake up in the middle of the night—"

"I know," Mabel interrupted him. "I can't sleep when you can't sleep. Maybe you just need to talk to me."

"I don't want to tell you Mabel," Harry said.

"Look, I'm tough, I can handle it."

"No, no you can't!" Harry snapped and walked out to the lawn. "I'm going to get the Chevy off the blocks. Going to ask Tom for some help."

Then he started to drink—at first it was just a beer here and there. Seemed okay on a Friday night after a long work week. Then he needed one to get through the weekend. It evolved into a routine. After work to where he knew the beer was always cold. Around the corner from the Farm & Fed, Harry walked to VFW Post 3432. He felt compelled to be there with men who shared much of his own experience. Those who were the forgotten ones. The ones that the war didn't destroy but were injured were given parts of their skin and body parts back to them in order to return home and walk among the living. It was cruel but an effective way for soldiers to pretend to be normal.

But there was nothing normal about them. There was nothing normal about Bobby Fogerty's withered hand. He was feeding a cartridge belt into a Madsen, "And the damn thing ate my hand!"

Nothing normal about Jack Yudishak who was left with half his face. Too close to a grenade and not enough skin to properly stitch it together. His wife left him because it was just too hard to look at him.

And nothing normal about the demons that crept into Harry's dreams. The monsters of his damaged interior where a ricocheted bullet tore up his insides so badly, appeared as soon as he closed his eyes. The surgeons took his spleen and a yard or so of his intestines. They left him with pain and meager meds to heal. But the infection ruined him even further, the sulfa drugs gave him headaches, fatigue and nightmares that he couldn't escape. Nothing normal about the soldiers—the former residents of the town of Pine Grove.

The area CCC camp was abandoned. Having served their purpose, the camps where the men worked, before they joined the war. And then those workers died or returned home to jobs at the lumber mill or the steel mill or the mines. Part of the camp was returned to nature by the forest service. Another part was bought by the Boy Scouts to use to train them in the manly arts of outdoor life. It will never train them for anything like trying to build a fire amongst the ice-coated trees of the Ardennes. How to bury dead soldiers who were alive and talking to you one second and blasted through the head, the next. Or how to re-enter life without any preparation for how much the world changed while you were hunkered down in a trench. Harry needed to return to something normal.

And that normal was farming.

The farms always need extra hands but machinery and technology shortened a man's day. Tractors, combines, harvesters and even silos had been upgraded and improved.

The only thing that was a constant for Harry was the smells. The farm still stank of manure in summer, smelled like burning leaves in fall, smelled of smoky wood fires and mince pie in winter and smelled of fresh mowed grass in spring. The smell of dirty muddy dogs, soiled diapers, Mabel's butter cakes and even Mabel; these smells reoriented him to the life he remembered and dreamed about.

Mabel still nagged him to spend more time with the kids. "Harry, they're growing up so fast," she said. "You'll turn around one day and they'll be gone off and married."

She was right. Their oldest Susan was driving their tractors and begging for the old Chevy to come off the blocks. Their son Eddie was in love with the girl next door, the next in line, Dana, was mooning over boys in her school and younger sister, Karen, teased Dana mercilessly about her flirting and baby, Lillian wasn't a baby any more. Lillian was walking, done with breast feeding and saying "Daddy" and "Mama". Lillian was even sitting at the table feeding herself, no more sitting in a high chair. This morning Mabel reminded him of the Great Oak Tree they stood under before he was deployed. "Remember that big old tree? It put down roots Harry, we're putting down roots, too. But you gotta go water your roots, you know?" She nodded towards the children. *A man's gotta water the roots of his dynasty or it'll die out,* he thought.

Time to get out of his rut. Time to drive the Chevy. Time to move on.

Slowly but surely things returned to a rhythm. The earth never let Harry forget who he was. No matter how much innocence he or the world lost, he still had children to raise, a farm to run, and coal to dig. The world could speed by but the clouds always drifted slowly. The rain always came, the snow always blew in the windows and sun always came out after the storm. Some things never changed and thank God for that.

1946

The funeral was well-attended. There were two types of attendees, those who were genuinely sorry that Jan Herrstadt drowned in the mining accident. And those who were just curiosity seekers. But everyone wanted to look like they cared, thought Harry. Until last week no one even knew you could drown in a mine. All you heard about were collapses or falls. But now the mines were going deeper. Richer veins of coal seemed to be hidden thousands of feet below the surface. Unfortunately, for every ton of coal, there had to be almost 30 tons of water pumped out of the mine. Whole lakes were formed from the forced evacuation of the water from pumps. Jan's death occurred on the day the pump gave out. The water back-flowed with such force, it knocked him back against the wall of the tunnel. He was most likely dead before he was submerged, the coroner told the family. "Oh, I think his number was up," said his father. "It's never where you're going to die, it's just when."

Harry felt Jan's death to his core. The Mars family had dirty fingernails coming out of the womb. They were farmers or miners. They dug the soil every day of their lives and there wasn't shame in it. After the mine strikes, pay increased and there was some lip service to safety protocols, but nothing got safer. Technology was available, but never utilized. There was a whole new Bureau of Mining established. All sorts of permits and forms now had to be filled out, regulations followed, hearings to attend and public notices to be read by the miners. All these things slowed mining down but not much safer. But the regulations sure made bureaucrats fat and happy.

There was talk about a Conowingo Tunnel that was to be the underground water way they would divert all the water into the Conowingo River in Maryland. They had planned it for a while. But right now, the blueprints were just sitting on someone's desk. And some kid like Jan was going to drown tomorrow. And there would be more funerals. And no one would care.

After the funeral, Mabel and the kids went home. Harry found himself with his brother-in-law Tom having a beer at the Tuplehocken Rod & Gun Club.

"Don't worry," Tom consoled Harry. "The world is going get better."

"Oh yeah? From what I see things are getting worse," Harry said. He looked around the room. The men in the room were war alumni and members of the club. The mood was somber. I'm not the only one with demons, thought Harry.

"No, no," Tom insisted. "There's a lot of good things coming our way. Here's what I think—" Tom was interrupted by a chair being knocked over. Karl Delliker was staggering over towards them.

"Hey! Hey you," Karl yelled pointing at Tom. "Where the hell were you?"

"Whaddya mean?" Tom was confused. "I was at the funeral. But I was—"

"No!" Karl yelled, now in front of Harry and Tom. "The war, you idiot! You were never deployed, were you?"

"The hell I wasn't," Tom responded, anger growing. "I was stationed in Hawaii."

"After the bombin' I heard," Karl was breathing heavily on both men. He was swaying, his body infused with alcohol. "You coward! Comin' in after the fights over!"

"Hey, Karl, that's enough," Harry stood up and put his hands on the man's shoulder and moved him back a few feet away from Tom. "Time to go home."

Karl pushed back and staggered towards Tom. "Fight's not with you Harry. It's with your yellow coward of a brother-in-law."

"Hey, shut up!" Tom yelled. He reached for Karl, but Harry stood in his way.

Harry kept his voice low. "Don't you ever call my brother-in-law a coward, got it, Karl?"

"Ah, you shut up, too," Karl said and made a clumsy swing at Harry. "You're a…a…jackass anyways."

Harry shoved Tom aside and said, "Apologize, Karl."

"Not on your life," Karl sneered.

Harry planted his feet and launched his left fist at Karl's mouth. The blow jerked Karl backwards, but he remained standing.

"Apologize," Harry repeated.

Karl's answer was to swing wildly in Harry's general direction. He landed a few fists on Harry's arm, but nothing to slow Harry down in the least. Harry pummeled Karl until the man sunk to the ground. Blood seeped from Karl's right eye, mouth and left ear. His eyes rolled back in his head and sputtered, "Nuff, nuff."

Tom pulled Harry away. "Apologize Karl."

"Sorry," gasped Karl. "Sorry."

The patrons and bartenders who held their collective breaths during the bloody exchange sighed in relief. "Prop him up," the bar tender ordered. Karl's drinking buddy doused him with cold water.

Harry and Tom left without paying for their drinks. There was no need. Their table had a stack of ones nestled by their empty mugs, donated by a grateful brotherhood, who never tolerated disrespectful jackasses. It was the brotherhood of servicemen who respected each other no matter in which arena (Europe or Pacific) they fought. A few GIs like Karl tried to make one arena a deeper hell than the other. Germany had surrendered on May 7, 1945, the war in the Pacific had continued until after the atomic bombings of Hiroshima on August 6, 1945 and Nagasaki August 9, 1945 and the world waited for Japan to surrender. Then on September 2, 1945 aboard the USS Missouri, Japan signed the official surrender.

In bed that night, Mabel stroked Harry's abdomen and ran her hand along the long vertical scar. She burst into tears.

"Stop Mabel," Harry said. "I'm okay, that fight didn't hurt me none. Plus, I'm healed up and stitched up, thanks to Uncle Sam. It's not like they took my soul or anything like that."

"What did they take?" Mabel asked. "It's an awfully big scar."

"Well, let's see, they took my spleen, and I think a few feet of gut," he paused, "and I think they took out a lung, a kidney, part of my liver and some of my bladder." He paused again. "But I saved my heart for you," he laughed.

"Stop it," she reprimanded him. "But did they really take all that?"

"No, no, Mabel, I was pulling your leg," he said holding her tight. "I'm all here; whatever they took out, so help me, I don't need it." He kissed her forehead. "Come on, let's work on baby number six."

The true fact is that Harry was very lucky to be alive. The surgeons never saw a person with Harry's condition survive. A good portion of his small intestines was ischemic and had to be removed. The army surgeons cut and removed a few feet of his small intestines and performed one of the first anastomosis of the small intestines. Harry's prognosis was grim and if he did survive, he probably would not be able to work or live long.

CHAPTER FOURTEEN

*"Every little bird in the tall oak tree ... flapping them wings
sayin' go bird go. "*
    – Bobby Day, Rockin' Robin, 1957

When lunch was over, Lillian looked at Dan. "Well?"
"Well, what?"

"What's your idea to make the tree last almost forever?"

"Almost forever," corrected Dan.

"Whatever. I bought you lunch and now I am waiting."

"Okay, okay," he conceded. "So, Gilly and Ken and I, have been kicking around the idea of milling the wood and using it to make all sorts of things—mementos, plaques, some small furniture and that sort of thing."

"That's wonderful."

"Also about 15 to 18 years ago, someone collected some of the acorns from the Great Oak, grew saplings and then had a sapling sale. One of the saplings was planted at the church and is now about 15 feet tall. Pastor Tom told me that one of the members of the congregation planted one from the sale and it is still growing in their yard."

"Are the saplings producing acorns?" asked Lillian

"I'd like to grow a sapling and plant it in our yard, it would have the Great Oak's DNA," Lillian said.

"Speaking of DNA, how are things progressing with the family tree?"

"Well, it is very complicated and I am just two generations away from the Tilridges that are buried under the Great Oak Tree. I plan to ask Pastor Tom if I can search the church's burial records that are stored in the "Church Museum." "Maybe I can have the family tree completed by the time we have our family picnic."

"And you know even after we take the tree down, the stump will still be there."

"Really?"

"Yup. There's just no way, is there anyone at all going to be able to grind that stump. And it'll take a while for the roots to slowly rot away. Besides, I'm pretty sure Pastor Tom wants the stump to remain there for people to get an idea of how big the tree was."

"I'd like to see the Great Oak Tree again," Lillian said. "I'd like to touch it once more before you take it down."

"Don't worry you will," Dan assured her. "Maybe we'll get everybody to be there. A big family reunion."

"Oh, that would be wonderful!" Lillian cried. "I'll invite my aunts and we'll get all six of the kids and their families to see the Great Oak Tree."

***

Baby number six didn't survive. The miscarriage was as sudden and swift as the blizzard that howled through Pine Grove.

"Winter, this year is going to be tough," Mabel's mother warned her. "Best to take it easy." But Mabel couldn't take it easy. Harry was drinking again. He was still functional and able to work during the day, but at night, she did her best to stay out of his way. He was never out of control, but he was shouting at the top of his lungs. That kind of shouting made the kids nervous. It made them cry. For the most part, she herded the kids to bed early. She nagged the older ones to get on with their homework or finish up chores.

When Harry finally made it to bed, he snored 'til dawn. Then he'd managed to get coffee and head off to work. His contribution to the farm chores, house repairs and raising the children was usually on the weekends. During the week, knowing the farm wasn't going to take care of itself, Mabel and the kids pumped the water, fed the animals, cleaned the house and made the meals. The older children helped with the dishes and taking care of the younger siblings when Mabel was tending to the barn chores. She was exhausted half the time. The older kids were rambunctious and the younger ones were into everything. School was a break, but still Mabel found herself taking on so much because Harry was unable or unavailable to help.

It was a bitter cold morning and when Mabel went to milk the cow, she found the barn gate had frozen shut. She tugged so hard she became overheated from her effort. She needed a man's strength, but her son Eddie was on his way to school. Harry was at work. She tugged and tugged and the pain that shot up her spine took her breath away. Mabel, hunched over, made her way back to the house and filled the hot water bag and laid on it. She ordered, in her sharpest tone, her 5 year old Karen to watch and play with Lillian. Lillian dozed for a half hour and her back felt better when she sat up. Karen and Lillian were by her side playing with their toys. The older children (Susan, Eddie and Dana) returned home from school and it was time to milk the cow again. That evening the barn gate opened, the afternoon sun had melted the ice on the hinge. The next day, stiff and sore, Mabel made sure that everything was running and kids ware making it to school and the younger ones were fed and washed up. When she went to milk the cow, the barn gate was frozen shut again. This time Mabel went back to the house and filled a pail with hot water.

She went back to the barn gate and poured the hot water over the hinge. The ice on the hinge melted and in haste to get the gate open, Mabel thrust her weight against the stubborn gate. Somewhere deep in her body she felt a tearing. Lord, she thought, hope it's not my back. But the burning pain in her lower gut told her no it was something more serious. She made it back to the house and to her surprise she saw Susan washing the faces of Karen and Lillian. Susan turned to her mother and said, "I was worried about you and I decided to stay home from school to help you." Mabel didn't object, in fact she was relived. Later she was consumed with a wave of nausea and cramping. Susan yelled to Karen to go get Grandma Mercer and bring her to them. Karen ran across the dirt lane to grandma's house. She didn't knock, she opened the door and yelled, "Something's wrong with mommy, come quick," she cried to her grandmother. Mabel's mother grabbed her coat and ran along after Karen.

The blood on the floor, startled Leah Mercer. She shooed the kids to the kitchen and told Susan to make a little lunch of apple butter and bread for her younger siblings and to heat some water.

Leah did her best to clean up Mabel. I'm sorry, I'm sorry Mabel apologized. I didn't even know.

"How can a woman not know she's pregnant?" Leah scoffed. "But no matter," she relented when she saw the sad look on her daughter's face. "I'll send Susan to get your dad and have him get Dr. Courtnor." Leah washed Mabel and then cleaned up the blood on the sofa and the floor. Leah and Mabel were happy to see Dr. Courtnor and his Midwife. The Dr. and the Midwife tended to Mabel, they were able to help deliver the tiny remnants of the baby. The midwife also quietly promised to bury the bambino with his placenta under a tree in a small pine box. Mabel was grateful to have someone with gentle hands and an empathetic sensibility. She told the midwife to say a prayer and if possible, put the name John on the box. She loved that name for a boy. It was simple and small.

Harry sensed something was wrong and at the end of his work shift, he didn't stop for drinks but went straight home. His mother-in-law met him at the door and told him about the miscarriage. Leah also gave him an earful about how Mabel is taking on everything, doing too much. Then Dr. Courtnor met with Harry and told him that Mabel had lost a lot of blood and would need to rest for several weeks. He also told Harry that Harry and Mabel should wait at least 6 months before trying to have another baby. "She needs time to heal," explained Dr. Courtnor. Harry took the rebuke from his mother-in-law seriously as his looked at his wife's face which was the color of limestone. He sat by Mabel's bedside for hours, as he watched her chest rise and fall. Her breathing was deep and slow.

"Mabel, I promise I'll quit the bottle," he whispered. "I'll stay home and help you with the kids."

The next day Harry true to his word, went to work late and he helped his mother-in-law get the kids off to school. He fixed the barn gate by greasing it, he gathered the eggs and shoveled a path to the back outbuildings. But as the winter thawed, Harry returned to the VFW drinking as much as he had before Mabel's miscarriage.

As the spring arrived. Mabel was once again managing children, the farm and trying her best to make sure the house stayed standing. Summer would be a relief and she just let the kids outside to play. Maybe she's lie down for a rest. It sounded like a good idea but it never happened.

1948

Things were looking brighter for Harry and Mabel in the spring of 1948. They had two wonderful surprises. First, Mabel was pregnant again and due in October. October is a beautiful month and both Eddie and Lillian were born in October. Susan was born in September, Karen was born in November and Dana shared the month of March with her Dad.

The second surprise was a visit from Uncle Eli Rink who was now 65 years old. Uncle Eli and Aunt Dawn were a breath of fresh air to Harry & Mabel. They were as lovely as the freshness of spring. Uncle Eli and Aunt Dawn planned to spend a week with Harry and Mabel. Every night after dinner, everyone gathered in the living room to hear stories of the Tilridge family, Tilridge Farm, the Johnstown flood and the Great Oak Tree. Only Harry and Mabel listened closely to what Uncle Eli was saying. Karen and Lillian still had short attention spans and the older children were more interested in the here and now not old stories of what used to be. Later in life all of Harry and Mabel's off springs would regret not having listened to Uncle Eli and never asking their Dad about the war. Uncle Eli and their Dad were walking history books.

For Harry and Mabel, the week ended for too quickly. Harry and Mabel promised to visit Uncle Eli in Basking Ridge. Uncle Eli was a terrific writer and he knew how to sniff out details of a story that other Journalists missed. The story that gave him the greatest challenge was the Tilridge family history. He spent many years researching records and talking to anyone who may have come in contact or heard about the Tilridge family. He complied all of his notes and records into a book and before heading for home, he gave a copy to Harry and Mabel. "You will find our family history to be quite complex and interesting in ways you would have never thought and how the Spirit of a Great Oak Tree played a key role in our lives," Uncle Eli stated as he handed a copy of his book to Harry and Mabel.

The foliage in October of 1948 was spectacular. And on crisp morning in the middle of the month, Mabel gave birth to a bouncing baby girl with dark hair and brown eyes. They named her Janet. Janet giggled and brought smiles to those around her. Everyone seemed to want to spoil her.

While Mabel was recovering from childbirth, she decided to read Uncle Eli's account of the Tilridge family. What she read was indeed interesting and yet troubling. It was going to be difficult to follow Grandpa Richard Tilridge's line back to Basking Ridge and her father-in-law's, Axel Tilridge Mars, line back to Basking Ridge and both lines back to the Great Oak Tree. Mabel decided that the children weren't ready for the family history lesson. Mabel stored the book in the family trunk.

1957

Lillian, now thirteen, had a huge teen crush on Alan Grande. A travelling Elvis look-a-like. He was tall, dark, lean and handsome. She was captivated by his voice and his charming smile.

"Isn't he dreamy?" she asked her older sister Karen, as she showed her a picture she had torn out of the local paper.

"Uh, he's like a hundred years older than you," her sister scoffed.

"So what? I can fall in love with anyone I want to."

That made her sister fall on her bed and laugh. "You're not even a grown-up girl yet," she giggled. "Never even got your monthly yet."

Lillian stuck her tongue out at her sister, not having a better response. She also had no idea why having your monthly was closely tied or even necessary to being able to fall in love.

Lillian promised herself she'd do something exciting before she headed into eighth grade. Earlier that day Lillian was able to corner Chrissy Heitzer at the pool. Chrissy listened to Lillian and her plans for that evening, but she needed an older more sophisticated person to help implement those plans. She explained to Chrissy that her sisters couldn't be bothered.

"Please?" Lillian begged. "My sisters are just big drips. They'll tell on me too!"

"Oh, alright," Chrissy conceded. "Make sure that you're at the little post by the gazebo before 8:30 sharp."

"I'll be there!"

Lillian sneaked out of the house to see Alan Grande play at the bandshell in The Eleanor Roosevelt Park. He was only there one night. It was her only chance to see him perform. She dressed up to look as grown up as her older sister.

It had been a rainy summer. The Wheat shot up so quickly, famers were tempted to harvest early. Lillian remembered her father and mother having a fight about it. Mom was saying wait, but Dad was saying no, he was worrying over the wheat. Conditions were perfect for the fungus—hot sticky and nothing was drying out. To make things worse, according to the radio and the old men down at the post office there was a hurricane on its way, Hurricane Audrey. Flooding and high winds were now being reported in faraway places like Texas and Charleston, South Carolina.

Betsy Smith said her oldest son called to say he wasn't able to get on the highway to travel up to visit for the weekend.

"Roads are all flooded something awful," she told Mabel. "I guess I won't see him this summer."

"Now you don't know that," Mabel said. "I'll bet it just blows over and he'll be up to see you in no time."

Lillian told no one of her nocturnal plans that evening. Dad wasn't even home from the VFW. Mom was worn out all the time, just trying to keep the household chores of cooking, cleaning, washing clothes and ironing along with helping with the farm work.

The wind blew occasional gusts, whipping the branches around like hands waving frantically in the air. Just as Lillian scooted through the window and slithered down the trellis, rain began to pour. She knew there was a lady's room at the park with mirrors so she felt confident she could repair her makeup.

Her plan was to meet up with Chrissy at the post by the gazebo and they'd both go sit together for the show. At least if one of them got caught, the other could vouch for her. Chrissy was going into ninth grade and was already being appraised by tenth grade boys. Lillian considered her as one of the most mature girls she knew. Truth be told she didn't know many other girls other than her sisters.

Chrissy was already wearing a bra too. Lillian swiped a bra from her sister's drawer and attempted to fill it out with tissues. To her humiliation, the tissues were wet and soggy before she even got to the park. She pulled them out, wadded them up and tossed them in the trash.

The rain had stopped but the wind still blew. The remaining wheat was ready to be harvested. It would turn into July

At the park, Chrissy was waiting by the post at the gazebo. "I thought you'd never show up!"

"I said I would and I did," Lillian replied. "And I'm early to boot."

"Oh hush, let's go in," said Chrissy.

Alan Grande appeared on stage and you would have thought it was The King himself. A half dozen females rushed to the foot of the bandshell and there was a more than generous applause from the audience. Lillian came to her feet immediately. She turned around but Chrissy and many of the other attendees were running in the aisles.

He sang, "Till I Waltz Again with You" and "My Happiness" and then he sang a brand-new song called, "Hound Dog" which the crowd went crazy for. The old timers were offended by the rock n roll music. Grande's crazy dancing didn't earn him any points with the old timers either. They complained loudly hoping the younger crowd would hear and heed, but Lillian thought, *who cares, he's so handsome.*

After the performance, Alan took a little break to meet with the locals. The girls flocked to him like moths to a flame; they couldn't help themselves. Lillian found herself among them, clearly the youngest and the least boy-savvy. Just as star-struck as the others.

They swarmed around him, asking a million questions. One of them gushed, "Oh isn't he the living end?" Lillian rolled her eyes and was squashed out of their circle. She walked over to his case and regarded his guitar.

"What kind of wood is it made of?" she asked, brushing its deep brown surface.

The swarming girls tittered. "What a stupid question," one of them remarked.

Alan picked up his guitar. "This old thing? It's made out of spruce," he said.

"Oh, is it from around here?"

"Well, no, it's from somewhere. It's pretty common, but it's got a good sound. I'm saving up for an electric guitar," he told her. "One made of swamp ash. I'm thinking of a Gibson, Les Paul or maybe a Fender Telecaster."

"Who are they?"

"Well," he laughed, "They aren't a who, as much as they are a what. They're guitar makers. They make all kinds of guitars for all kinds of music people."

"They make special guitars?"

"Yes, ma'am they do."

"Must cost a lot, huh?"

One of the swarming girls gave a grunt of disgust. "How rude!"

"Woo-boy, more than I've got now. But just you wait 'til I buy one," said Alan. "I'll be singing my own songs and playing bigger gigs."

"I hope you do," Lillian said. "Honest I do. A brand-new guitar on a great big stage."

"Well thank you, thank you very much," he said. "Hey what's your name?

"Um, I'm Lillian," she hesitated to give her full name, just saying her first name out loud sounded odd in her ears.

"That's a real pretty name."

Lillian was flustered. "Well, uh, oh, thank you, thank you very much," she repeated.

The girls around her tittered again. "Is she five?" one of the swarming girls whispered, loud enough for Lillian to hear.

Lillian never had a conversation this long with any man, not even her father. Especially about a topic she was curious about. She stole a glance over at the concession stand. Chrissy was talking to two boys that were in her class at school. The boys had leers on their faces and they were eyeing her up and down. Chrissy was wearing her poodle skirt, white Peter Pan collar blouse and a bright blue scarf. She was so put together;

her ensemble was perfect. And I look like a farm girl, thought Lillian. With an emphasis on girl.

"It was nice talking to you Mister Grande." she said feeling stupid for not have anything more interesting to say. To her utter shock Alan leaned down and gave her a little kiss on the cheek. "Good bye sweetheart, stay sweet."

There were gasps from the swarming girls, who looked at each other dumbfounded.

Lillian's cheek felt so warm and sweet, she put a hand to her face and promised herself, *I'll never wash this side of my face again.*

She stumbled away and gave Alan a little wave. Then met up with Chrissy. "Ugh, those boys were being so brazen." "I am ready to go home," Chrissy stated. The next act was a barber shop quartet and neither Chrissy nor Lillian were interested in staying.

"So, what's wrong with you?" she asked.

"Nothing," Lillian lied. She was ready to burst into tears of joy. *A boy kissed me. No. A young man kissed me.*

"You're just being silly," observed Chrissy. "Ugh, this wind is ruining my hair."

"At least it stopped raining," Lillian tried to be optimistic. The glass was definitely half full. In fact, it was brimming over. As if on cue the rain began to fall in sheets.

On their way home Chrissy complained bitterly. The roads were running streams. Debris and branches had fallen in the middle of the road, forcing the girls to take a longer route home. Chrissy who lived closer was drenched and exhausted. She walked into her house through the front door. "I don't care if they yell at me," she gasped. "I just want to get dry and go to bed."

Lillian walked the next half-mile by herself in the rain wind and dark. The faces that greeted her at the front door were scowling. "I just want to get dry," Lillian said and she burst into tears.

The next morning, she awakened to whispers of, "You're gonna die." and "Mom and Dad are going to kill you." Lillian trudged downstairs and decided to face the music. But nothing was said about her violation of curfew. She was informed quietly over milk and toast that the Heintzelman's youngest, Joey, was drowned in their pond. Apparently, Lillian wasn't the only one who thought it would be fun to go out and play in the middle of a hurricane.

CHAPTER FIFTEEN

"I fear you'll find that love is like the lovely lemon tree."
— The Lemon Tree, Will Holt, 1959

"Are you ready?"

"For what?"

"To grow an oak of your own," Dan said.

"Really?"

"Yeah, come on," Dan grabbed the bill. "Let's see what Ken and Gilly are up to. We'll figure out how to get the Gobin clan over there for the take down. It's going to take a few days to get the tree on the ground, then haul the logs over to the mill and see what's unusable."

"Isn't it all usable? I mean it's so huge you could make a house from it, right?"

"No, Mom, remember the center is all filled with cement. And the branches, well even though they are large, won't make much more than a piece of furniture or two."

"That's all?"

"Mom, you gotta understand, the tree has serious decay, that's why Ken and Gilly are using the ultrasound. They need to know where to cut, or not to cut. The tree could crumble into pieces and then it's all over."

"Wow, it's that dangerous?"

"Oh yeah, the cabling and the plates are probably rusted into the tree. Those are the first things to remove."

"And then?"

"Next they'd drop the branches and cut up the smaller branches for laser cutting. Then the larger branches."

"What about the trunk and the roots?" Lillian asked.

"Talking about roots, mom, how are you doing with proving that we are descendants of the Tilridges' who are buried under the tree?' asked Dan reluctantly.

"I thought you would never ask," replied Lillian.

"I was able to trace your great grandfather Axel Tilridge Mars back to Jeremy, Sarah and baby Martha Tilridge whose gravestones are here under the tree. It took a lot of time and I had to use court records of marriages, births and property deeds; Census records; church records and even a genealogy site online." "However, I am at a standstill with tracing your great grandmother Elizabeth Rink Mars and her parents back to Basking Ridge. I do know that your great grandfather Richard and grandmother Sachi were in the Johnstown flood and that is when they became the step-parents of Elizabeth and Eli Rink. Richard and Sachi Tilridges' lines are very complicated. Judging from notes in the Basking Ridge Church records, I am certain that they were also buried here and I believe Richard had something to do with the sea shell that Pastor Tom mentioned." "While I was searching through your great grandmother Elizabeth's records, I had a flashback to my youth. I was only four years old and Uncle Eli visited us. He talked about the old days the whole time he and Aunt Dawn were with us. I was too young to understand what he was saying. I also remember something about a book he wrote. Also your dad and I heard about a Tilly Tilridge when we honeymooned on Salt Cay. She was a legend among the locals. Dad and I should have looked into her story but we had other things on our minds," explained Lillian with great satisfaction.

"Mom, it all sounds very interesting and one day I want to hear all the details, just not today. You can continue your research while I think of ways to keep the spirit of the Great Oak Tree alive." "Now, to get back to where I left off about the trunk."

"The best for last," Dan said. "They'll have to dissect that carefully. But you'll see it all first hand. Time to make some phone calls."

1957

Lillian, along with her family and most of the town of Pine Grove, attended Joey Heintzelman's funeral. It seemed as if all they ever did was go to funerals.

After she got home, her sister Karen gave her a what-for. "How could you be so stupid?" her sister hissed. "Mom and Dad had an awful row!" They were worried sick about you.

"You should have told somebody where you were," growled Dana. "You could've told me."

Lillian stood her ground. "No, I couldn't tell either of you. Because neither of you would have kept it a secret. And it's not like either of you have never sneaked out of the house before."

Her older siblings were silent.

"Come on, Lil' you could have died!" Her sister Dana took a different tack.

"Yeah, it could have been you they fished out of the pond," her sister Karen piled on.

"I was fine."

"You were not."

"Was too."

"You didn't care about anybody but yourself," her sister Dana accused. "Made everyone worry. Dad and Mom were fighting really badly." An AWOL daughter probably sent him over the moon.

"And after everything Mom's been through," her sister Dana added.

Lillian couldn't argue. Her selfishness did cause a stir. "Well, I'm here and I'm alive. Thank you very much."

"You're lucky," her sister Dana proclaimed.

"When Gram got here and told Dad and Mom about Joey, Dad looked like he was going to throw up."

"Then they went searching for you."

Lillian did feel badly. She hadn't meant for her parents to be as concerned and worried as they were. She thought in her child's reasoning that since there were so many kids in the house, they wouldn't notice if one was gone.

She hadn't meat to be selfish. She just wanted to see Alan Grande. She knew her mother wouldn't allow it.

After the funeral service, Lillian screwed up the courage to approach her mother. They had been keeping their distance for almost three days. Her mother was standing outside, all by herself, next to the cemetery gate. Lillian's father had driven his mother home, now that Gramma Leah was having back pain when she went walking, Dad drove her everywhere.

"Mom, I'm sorry," Lillian mumbled. She stood so close to her mother she could smell both lilac water and bacon grease, her mom had made baked beans for the Heintzelman's. Providing food for the family of the deceased was a Pine Grove tradition.

Mabel nodded towards the mound of fresh dirt. "It could have been you."

Lillian looked at her mother. The pain in Mabel's eyes was real and raw. No one wanted to lose a child, most especially a young one. And her mother's loss of a baby not yet born, made it worse. Lillian didn't say anything because there was nothing to say. She leaned her head against her mother's shoulder. She felt her mother's bones jutting through the thin fabric. Mom never took enough time to eat the wonderful meals she had prepared and she never got enough sleep.

Lillian felt even worse just thinking about it.

"You should say something to your father," Mabel said. "He was so worried."

"I will, Mom, I will."

"Listen to me Lillian," Mabel said. "You never breathe a word of what I'm going to tell you, do you hear?"

Lillian nodded; eyes wide.

"When your grandmother came to tell us, they found someone floating in the pond, we were all in the kitchen Dana, Karen and Janet (Susan was married and lived in the Midwest and Eddie was in the Air Force)—the only person who wasn't there, was you."

Lillian gulped.

"Your father ran up to your room," Mabel said. "He was yelling when he couldn't find you. Asking everyone where you were. He gave Susan a good shake, threw a chair and the noise made Janet cry and he yelled at me too." Mabel smiled. "And of course, I yelled back."

"Sorry," Lillian whispered. "I know you hate to fight."

"I do, I hate it, but I had to yell back, he was saying pretty awful things. So, I yelled. A lot."

Mabel put her arms around Lillian. "You have to know you helped your dad quit his drinking. The idea of losing you—any of you kids--made him straighten up and fly right."

Lillian folded herself into her mother's arms and sobbed. "I'll never do it again, I promise!"

Mabel kissed Lillian's head. "No don't make a promise like that. You've got lots of years ahead of you. How 'bout you make a promise that you'll at least let me know that you're heading out? Alright then, promise me?"

Lillian nodded sniffling. "Promise."

Two years later, Lillian kept her promise to her mother. A nearly grown up fifteen-year-old, she whispered, "going to Jenny's for a little while." And she slid out the door.

Her mother nodded. Lillian heard, "Door's locked at 10:30."

Jenny Bradford was the richest girl in town. She was also the ugliest. She was picked on at school. Lillian felt sorry for her. No matter the kind of money her parents invested in her—wardrobe, braces, eyeglasses to remove her perpetual squint, skin doctors for her pimples--she never got any prettier. Lillian told the kids to quit picking on Jenny at lunch. From then on Lillian was Jenny's hero.

Lillian's parents didn't approve of Jenny. "She's too snooty," her mother said. But Lillian knew Jenny's taciturn demeanor wasn't from being, what her father called, "a rich snob," but an inability to socialize. Jenny Bradford rarely spoke to anyone except her parents and her teachers. She just didn't know how to have a conversation. Her mother would say, "Hello Jennifer" and Jenny would look like a startled doe, say "hi" and then run. When Jenny and Lillian talked, she was like any other teenage girl. They chatted about music and boys and school and plans for the future. Jenny wanted to go to college. She had her heart set on being the next Amelia Earhart.

"Wait a minute, they never found her body," Lillian reminded Jenny.

"That's not going to happen to me," Jenny assured Lillian. "I just want to fly or maybe I'll be an engineer. Just like my dad." Mr. Bradford was a geology engineer with the Pennsylvania Mining Department. Her mother was a teacher at Lycoming Community College. Lillian hated to admit she didn't have a deep desire to go to college. She just wanted to get through high school. That seemed daunting enough. But she offhandedly said, "I think I want to be a tennis player."

"Yeah, you're really good at sports." Jenny offered her support. "Or you can teach people how to play tennis. You're really good at helping little kids."

"Yeah, hey yeah, maybe a teacher," Lillian said.

As her classmates dropped out of school, faded into the myriad cliques of upperclassmen and graduated, Jenny and Lillian remained friends and kept in touch with each other.

Lillian did notice her mother was more relaxed. Her father rarely went back to his Friday habit of VFW drinking. He had stopped drinking except for picnics and birthdays, which were infrequent. A lot of promises were made the day after Joey Heintzelman's funeral. The summer prior to Joey's death, the church picnic was short and not so sweet because someone from town wanted to "get even" with her father. Lillian turned her head and POW, the guy poking her father's chest was on the ground. Harry, now having a reputation for being a tough guy, the Mars Family wasn't always the first ones invited to the local parties.

1960s

As the fabulous fifties melted into the chaotic sixties, Lillian passed into a brief flirtation with Roy Orbison. Her sisters and friends sang all his songs, *Only the Lonely, Crying, Running Scared and* etc.

Lillian's oldest sister Susan and her brother Eddie were married and raising families, her sister Dana had her heart set on moving to New York City, Karen just wanted to get married and younger sister Janet was in Jr High. Ever since Jenny told Lillian that she was good with kids, she puzzled over the idea of sports and teaching. Pine Grove was relatively safe from the divisiveness of cultural and political upheaval. Lillian decided to stay in her home state and go to Bloomsburg University. She decided this in her senior year in high school. It made sense. It was about two hours or so from her home. She worked at the Sure-Fine grocery store to save money for college. She took up the sports of tennis, basketball and cross country. She was often dismissed as a kid without any stamina because she was so slender. But Lillian realized you didn't' have to be a big muscular football player to have the kind of endurance and hand-eye coordination that most sports required. Both her parents had been active all their lives.

And they passed those genes on to Lillian.

Her upbringing gave her muscles a lot of practice. On a farm, there was always something to do. Something to lift, haul, feed or milk. Her mother also expected her help with her younger sibling. Jenny was right, she did get along well with kids who were younger than her. She rarely lost her temper, she was frustrated, yes, but never angry enough to swat and kick like the bigger kids at school would do. Even to their own siblings. Lillian's mother warned her that if she ever saw any older sibling beating the young, she was to go tell the teacher. They could call her a snitch if they wanted, but it was never ever permitted for an older brother to swat a little sister in the head. "Means that they get it from their parents."

Not that Lillian never got a spanking when she was young, she did. Not because if disobedience but because of her back sass. She was ready and able to defend herself even if meant going toe to toe with someone like her father. As she grew older, those actions dwindled and disappeared. Mostly because she and her father rarely crossed paths. Between school, chores and sports, she only laid eyes on him before going to bed. Sunday was the only day for family time.

In high school Lillian threw herself into everything. Grade school felt so far away, here, she was as ready to learn as ever. Learn about geography, and how far away Pine Grove was from Philadelphia. She loved her cross-country practices. Running through the soft woods that encircled the school, helped clear her head about biology. And with tennis, it was the best thing for her competitive spirit to smash the ball over the net. And the look on the opponent's face was also pretty satisfying. Lillian never attended her prom. It wasn't because she wasn't liked by the boys in her senior grade, she explained to those that asked that she wasn't interested in dancing. As much as she loved music and even played the clarinet in the school band, she couldn't dance. It was embarrassing to admit it. Her pride could not bring herself to admit that she didn't want the kids at her school to remember her as a klutz. As good as she was in sports and studies, she was uncoordinated in the movement of her body to the rhythm of music.

It was no surprise that Lillian was able to obtain partial scholarships to Bloomsburg College. She received the Rotary Club's Athlete of the Year Scholarship and The Ladies of Pine Grove Women's Auxiliary Award. She decided to be undeclared as the she went into her freshman year but was leaning toward education and sports health.

As Lillian headed though her junior year at college, she was able to take an overnight trip with her tennis team to Binghamton to play the college team there. It was there she met Tom Frenna. An architecture major and tennis player at Binghamton. She and Tom hit it off like two old chums talking about everything from the weather to the music on the radio. There was a new group from England that was taking America by storm. They were the Beatles and their records and albums were selling like hot cakes. Lillian and Tom sang along to songs like *"Eight Days a Week", "All my Loving" and "Help"* as they heard them on the radio. Lillian was so sure Tom was "the one" that she brought him home to Pine Grove to meet her parents. On Friday evening, the families went to a concert at the newly renamed JFK Memorial Park. To her surprise, Alan

Grande was performing. It was an odd homecoming to see him again. He was older, grayer and more somber, but oddly more peaceful. He was singing folk songs written and song by Arlo Guthrie and some of his own songs.

Grande shook Lillian and Tom hands after the concert. Alan didn't remember Lillian. She thought he wasn't as charming and energetic as he once was. Perhaps the Vietnam War weighted on him. He was playing a Martin D-18, a newer model. But it looked like it had weathered some miles.

Lillian confided in her mom about her feelings for Tom. Her mother was skeptical. "First loves are not the last loves."

Lillian felt stung. Tom was perfect, what was wrong with him? "Oh, mother what would you know? You only dated Dad. I mean you were practically married out of high school. Tom isn't Dad and I'm not you."

Her mother shrugged and said, "I know a good man when I see one."

Lillian wanted to defend Tom. As if he weren't good enough! Her father joined them and their conversation was cut short. "He seems like a nice fella," her father told them as he glanced over his shoulder. Lillian felt triumphant. She wanted to say, See? Dad thinks he's nice.

"Plays the guitar really well."

"What? Tom doesn't play the--," Lillian stopped. Her father wasn't talking about Tom, he was talking about Alan Grande. Lillian couldn't look at her mother. She went to retrieve Tom who was talking to some of the musicians that were relaxing in between sets.

Lillian and Tom cut their visit short and headed back to Bloomsburg. Tom sensed that Lillian was upset but he didn't pry. He talked about music and the two listened to some news in silence. Tom kissed her goodbye and headed back to Binghamton. "Don't worry," he said and drove away. Lillian was dismayed at his early exit. She wanted to talk to him about her parents' stoic behavior. She wanted to apologize for them and for herself. But she struggled with the words.

Her parents were the most honest people on the planet, why had they not seen in Tom what she saw? Tom was funny, charming and a talented debater. Everyone wanted to talk to him about his ideas. He was never at a loss for words. He was a busy young man. He had joined several clubs at Binghamton and often the two were unable to see each other for weeks. She had been dreaming about the kinds of things she'd do after college—maybe move to another city, start teaching, get married. Tom wanted to on to grad school. Marriage was a long way off for him. He saw his future in buildings, towers, skyscrapers. There was a need for people in architecture in Philadelphia or New York or maybe overseas, Paris or Singapore. "There's always some sort of structure that needs to be built," he told Lillian. "And I want to build it."

Lillian adored his passion for travel and building, but it just didn't leave time for them as a couple. "I'm swamped," he told her on the phone. "I'm going to hang up, finish my Lit paper, head to the Young Republicans Club and then off to tennis practice."

"You're working awfully hard," Lillian said. "You'll fall asleep in class if you don't slow down."

"I'll be fine, don't worry."

"But your birthday is tomorrow," Lillian reminded him. "It's Saturday too." She hoped he'd get the hint.

"I know I'm sorry," he laughed. "I'll light up a little candle. Yeah, my schedule tomorrow is just as helter-skelter as today." They chatted a little more and then said goodbye and hung up.

Poor guy, he has no plans for his birthday, Lillian thought, what can I do for him? She decided she'd surprise Tom. *What a great idea*, her friends gushed at the plan. So romantic too. Lillian bought him a book on the history of drafting and wrapped it up with tissue paper. The following day, she borrowed her friend's car and off she went to Binghamton.

Lillian was also surprised that day. As she pulled into Tom's dorm area, the Centre Quad at Binghamton, there was Tom in the center on a park bench surrounded by some of his buddies with his arm around a blonde. They were all singing, "Happy Birthday."

Lillian, too stunned to speak, pulled into a parking spot at the other end of the Quad. In her rearview mirror she saw Tom kiss the pretty blonde soundly on the lips. Her heart sunk and she hung her head and cried. He didn't even notice me, she thought. Of course, Tom didn't see her because he wouldn't have recognized her friend's car. And his attention was otherwise engaged. After sobbing through the handkerchiefs in her purse, she was able to pull herself together. If this was a tennis match, no matter how badly I was beat, I'd still run to the net and shake hands and let it go. But something beneath her skin roiled up and she opened the car door.

She strode toward the partiers on the park bench.

"My name is Lillian Mary Mars, and I'll be damned if some flutter bum is going to get the best of me!" She threw the gift-wrapped book at Tom's head, turned and drove all the way back to Bloomsburg. There she gave her friend the car keys and said, "I hate Binghamton."

Lillian poured herself into her studies and sports and stayed away from men. In her last year at Bloomsburg, all education majors with a concentration in athletics were assigned to study the construction of a school or gymnasium. Part of Lillian's senior paper was to see how air circulation, windows and ceiling fans benefitted student athletes' performance. It was, of course, a given that kids played better with better air circulation. Lillian did observe that when windows were open with "fresh" air circulating students did perform slightly better than when windows were closed and ceiling fans were spinning.

One of the workmen on the crew, Brian Gobin, was the go-to man that the foreman referred all the students to. Brian, who was tall, tough and quiet, had already graduated with a degree from Williamsport Area Community College in Construction Management. He was knowledgeable and able to give Lillian and the other students working on the project, valuable information. He was able to provide specs about window size, south-facing versus north-facing buildings and the sun's effects on heating or cooling large areas like a gym. Since he barely said anything to her when not in a group, she was shocked when he asked her just as she was leaving if she'd like to have a cup of coffee with him. "Unless you have a husband or boyfriend?"

Lillian smiled. "No boyfriend, but I'm really not dating anyone until after I get my degree."

Brian smiled back "Good idea. I'll see you in a few weeks."

"Okay, see you then." Lillian laughed to herself. He doesn't even know where I live or anything. How's he going to see me in a few weeks?

Graduation was bittersweet. Lillian said her goodbyes and moved back home. Her goal was to teach in nearby Irving. She had already contacted the high school principal. Mr. Norman Bennett sent notices to Bloomsburg and other teaching colleges about the need to fill three teaching slots and two girls' team coaching positions. With any luck, Lillian would secure one teaching and one coaching position.

Her first big Sunday meal at home, her mother asked for her help in setting the table. It surprised her because her younger sister Janet was old enough now to set the table. Janet would be graduating in a few weeks. Janet had probably made dinner on a few occasions while Lillian was away at college. But every once in a while, her mother looked out the window.

"A few extra people are coming," her mother said.

"Oh yeah? Gram? Dana? Karen? Eddie?"

"No, Gram doesn't get out much anymore. Dana is in NYC but Karen might come up later this weekend."

"Mom, who is it? Come on tell me," Lillian became irritated at her mother's uncharacteristic cryptic silence.

Her mother looked out the kitchen window. "Your father's talking to someone."

Lillian turned and saw Brian Gobin chatting with her father on the front porch. Lillian's jaw hung open for a minute. She collected herself and in her typical defensiveness, she confronted Brian on the front steps. "What in the world are you doing here?"

"I figured I'd come down and ask you out for a cup of coffee," he said. "You remember you said, see you in a few weeks."

Lillian stared at her father who just shrugged. "Or he can stay for dinner." If this were Tom, Dad would have scowled him all the way back to Bloomsburg, Lillian thought.

Brian did stay for dinner. And after six months of getting adjusted to her family, Brian proposed. Lillian's new teaching job, along with her head coaching position of girls' basketball, was a handful to manage. And planning a wedding nearly drove her insane. She wanted something small, but the Gobin clan wanted something large. Her father only said keep it simple and requested that the reception be held at the Pine Grove Banquet Hall. It wasn't too expensive and Lillian secretly put a deposit down to help her parents with the costs. Her wedding dress was made by two of her aunts and the money she saved went towards the honeymoon to Salt Cay.

In short order Lillian had two sons (Adam and Jason) and still managed to take the Irving High School Girls basketball team to semifinals. The year her youngest turned one, the girls went to finals and won the All-State Championship for the first time in the school's history.

The boys grew up natural athletes and were naturally curious. As Lillian's mom put it, "They are a handful and a half." Winters were dedicated to sledding and snowman building, during the springs they helped "Pap" at the farm, during the summers they explored the creeks during the day after chores and in the evening they collected fireflies and threw stones up in the air to fool the small brown bats that circulated overhead. Fall was school and Halloween with the craziest costumes. Things were going so well. Then Brian lost his job at the Penn Bethel Construction Company.

CHAPTER SIXTEEN

*"I frequently tramped eight or ten miles through the deepest
snow to keep an appointment with a beech-tree, or a yellow
birch, or an old acquaintance among the pines."*
— Henry David Thoreau, 1846

"The best for last," Dan said. "They'll have to dissect that
trunk section carefully. But you'll see it all first hand." Dan
repeated.

He explained to his mother, "There's not much you'd get
out of it. You can't build a house from this tree. As nice as that
sounds."

"Why not?"

"Because when you frame out a house you use pine, oak is primarily used for interior woodworking,

"My guess from that tree—you're only going to get 1,500 board feet of usable lumber. But there are so many other things that can be made from the lumber. I mean the sky's the limit. Benches can be made for the preschool where Pattie (Dan's wife) attended and/or for the park in Basking Ridge. I can mill the larger branches into one of those block votive candle holder things and center pieces. Smaller branches can be milled to make cheese boards, placards and the like. If I mill it even thinner I can make bookmarkers, letter openers and tree ornaments. You can even use the saw dust to fill clear ornaments. Old timers crafted cigar boxes from wood scraps. Heck, I'll bet you could make a guitar," Dan said. "And of course, good wine and bourbon makers always use oak for barrels."

"It's really up to your imagination, mom. Whatever requires oak wood is how the tree's lumber can be utilized. And each item made from the tree can be laser stamped with a logo, name and dates of the tree's life span. It's an amazing process to keep the Soul of the Great Oak Tree alive," Dan stated with great enthusiasm.

Planning the tree's take down will most likely take six months. Every detail has to be attended to; every "i" dotted and every "t" crossed, to ensure the work goes off without any damage or injury.

Dan explained that tomography was used to identify where they can make major cuts without grinding into steel or cement. Additionally, we've done ground and aerial inspections to gauge which cables may be supporting loads and which is the best order to remove the massive limbs.

"Mom, how are you coming with the plans to have family members to the Great Oak before its take down?"

***

Brian came home after work. Lillian knew even before he set foot in the house, she knew. The way his shoulders slumped he walked like he was defeated. As an athlete, Lillian knew that look was the look of a person who was beaten and beaten soundly.

Things were going so well. Weren't they the envy of all the families in Pine Grove? Lillian with her jobs at the school, her two boys Dan and Jake, were good students, natural athletes and fun-loving.

Falls were filled with school and sports. Lillian and Brian were dedicated to their sons. If Lillian couldn't get to the boys' practices, Brian was able to get out early and cheer on the boys. Same with games and all other activities. It wasn't that they turned a blind eye to the boys' antics, but they were able to make sure that if their boys did something inappropriate from toilet papering the principle's house on Mischief Night to bringing a goat into school for the homecoming pep rally, the boys had to face the consequences. Today, thankfully the boys were at school and Lillian was at home nursing a cold, still marking papers. The boys wouldn't be home for two more hours.

Watching Brian walking from the truck to the house was painful for Lillian. She held her tongue. Brain was not a talker.

Lillian learned to keep her mouth shut and wait. She waited and her heart hurt to watch him struggle to find the words and to speak them.

Brian shook his head. He couldn't bring himself to utter the words. All he could tell Lillian was, "They've decided to move operations to Nashville." He couldn't say that a handful of crew members would stay on, he wasn't one of them. It stung so badly.

"You mean the city in Tennessee?" Lillian was incredulous. How could a Pennsylvania-created company, one that even had a Pennsylvania name in it, move south to such a different area? How could Penn Bethel Construction Company leave town? She wanted to process it all but it was too much.

After a few days the Gobin clan came together. Lillian's mom was able to help with the boys. A few neighbors were always showing up with food in hand. Some of the men in town did their best to give Brian leads in the construction industry but the economy was heading south quickly.

Bruce Siegel approached Brian. He needed a good foreman to run the lumber mill.

"I know it's not your specialty," Bruce admitted with his usual candor. "But I know that you can run a crew and you'll have the respect of the men who are working at the mill. My foreman, Bob, is retiring and I can't spend the time to train a new wet-behind the ears kid."

Brian felt waves of relief wash over him. "I'll talk to Lillian."

"It's not going to be high pay," Bruce added. "But I can give you a decent wage that will help you keep your assets that you earned being a dedicated and outstanding employee of Penn Bethel."

Brian and Lillian were more than grateful. It gave the Gobin's the shot in the arm they needed. The 1970s weren't going to be too bad after all. Then came Watergate, waiting lines for gas and the uncomfortable way to end the Vietnam War. Somehow, they muddled through. Lillian kept coaching and teaching. Brian became the head foreman at the lumber mill and he never went back to construction.

Once again by the end of the 90's, Lillian and Brian were enjoying a certain peace in their lives. Empty nesters now, they sold the large house and moved to a smaller one. Their boys now married to lovely women and things seemed to be going smoothly until Brian got a call from Dan. Grown men don't cry like that he thought. Tracy had cancer. It wasn't going to be anything she could beat. They weren't even going to attempt brain surgery.

***

Dan routinely visited his wife's grave. He tried mightily but even after two years, it was still difficult to smile. For the kids, he thought always for the kids, get your game face on and make sure they never see you cry.

As he was leaving the cemetery one day, he saw another man just about his age, heading to one of the new graves. He wanted to reach out and say, Buddy, I know what you're going through. It's like a truck runs over you every day. But you'll survive somehow, you'll survive." He saw the man's shoulders shake, he thought go ahead and cry, it's not good to keep it inside.

On his drive home, he tried hard to leave his grief at the cemetery. But it crept along home with him. He looked on the mantle and saw a picture of him and the boys and her. He forgot to move that one behind the others. Not to be completely gone, he didn't want all the memories erased but just distant, just far enough away that he wasn't slammed in the face when he came home. He picked up the framed photograph. They were happier times, fun times of water sports, laughter and sun. Now there was gray and mourning and rarely any smiles or emotion. And missing her, always missing her. He tucked the photo behind the others. The one of Adam and his college buddies and girlfriend and one of Jason and his crazy vo-tech school friends. In the process he knocked over another picture.

His wedding picture. *Where did that come from?* Happy faces, promising forever to love each other. The caveat to that promise was a positive diagnosis of glioblastoma multiforme. The most aggressive thing that could happen to a brain. It wasn't that they didn't have twenty amazing years together. Two sons, Adam and Jason, a mortgage and all the good milestones.

"Cancer sucks," he said aloud.

"What?" Adam asked.

Adam had stopped at the house to check on his dad.

"Nothing, nothing," Dan mumbled. "Just talking to myself." "When did you arrive?"

"Just a few minutes ago," Adam replied. "Taking to yourself has been happening a lot lately," Adam stated.

"Well, I'm getting old."

"Dad I think we need to get you on a vacation."

"No, I don't need to—"

"Yes, how about a day or two? Something to get you out of the house so that you aren't thinking about work or mom. Okay?"

Dan gave in. "Alright, what do you have in mind?"

"How about tubing down the Delaware?"

"No, that would kill me. That takes too long, beside the Delaware is pretty shallow. Tubing the Delaware River would kill me. I can't sit still. You know me. Besides, water ain't my thing."

"Uh, I disagree I just think you don't want to do that because it'll remind you of mom."

Dan stopped.

"Yeah, I said it." Adam faced his father. "Dad, it's okay, I can't pretend not to talk about her. Mom was a big part of my life. I visit the grave too. But Jason and I aren't kids anymore. We're grown up now. And you need to date or something. You can't be all about work."

"I'm not. I got a date."

"No Dad, Christmas parties are not dating. And you don't have any women in your life other than Gram and Laura who's like a billion years old."

Dan had to laugh at his son's reference to the once-a-month cleaning woman. "One day, Adam, you won't think 60 is so old."

"Whatever. I'm making the reservations for next Saturday—clear your calendar."

"But I've got two loads of—"

"No, you're going," Adam was resolute.

"I'm not going to have any fun," Dan tried to beg off.

"So? I will."

"Guess it's all about you, huh?"

"Yep. See you next week on the Pennsylvania side of the Delaware River."

It was a crazy hot summer day when Dan and Adam found themselves on the Delaware River, elbow to elbow with a crowd of people who had nothing better to do with three hours than to sit in an inner tube and float down a river at an incredibly slow speed.

Dan noticed her right away. A pretty redhead, talking to a younger woman. In a weak moment Dan thought I'll just float far away from them. But the current made their inner tubes bump into each other and after courteous introductions, Dan found out as much as possible about the redhead without getting too personal.

Her name was Pattie or Patricia to her mother who by the way was still living in New Jersey. The younger woman was her daughter Katie. And it turns out that Katie had a similar discussion with her mom as Adam had with Dan.

Dan and Pattie spent the rest of the day on the river together. Not wanting it to end, Dan had to figure out if he was going to make a relationship with someone who was 70 miles from his home. In the end, Pattie and Dan felt like yes, this relationship born on the river was worth it.

For almost a year they drove up and down the Garden State Parkway. They kept their relationship as under wraps as they could. Neither one told the kids until their two-year anniversary. Adam wasn't surprised. Jason was surprised, but pleased. "Oh Dad, I'm so glad you have someone to be with after being alone for so long."

"I'm glad too," Adam chimed in. "I'm wondering though what's wrong with her."

"You shut up," Dan said. "She's great and perfect for me."

They dated for five years and then Dan bought a modest ring and planned to propose while they went house shopping.

There couldn't have been a worse day to hunt for anything, let alone a home. All along the Delaware, water seeped over its banks and the flooding lent itself to traffic issues and detours. Dan and Pattie gave up house hunting as now they learned that a Hurricane was headed towards New Jersey. That night, October 29, 2012, Hurricane Sandy hit New Jersey. It made landfall under a full moon and at high tide. New Jersey sustained a great deal of damage. Storm surge and flooding along with sustained winds of 80 mph and gusts at 100 mph left many people with damaged homes, uprooted trees and no electric.

The next day Dan and Pattie drove into the town of Basking Ridge to see if Sandy left her mark on the town. Basking Ridge was high on their house shopping list.

Many roads and streets were closed and there were downed trees everywhere. Dan and Pattie held their breath. Did the Great Oak Tree by the church survive? Dan managed to find a way to the church. To their great surprise and delight, the

Basking Ridge Great Oak Tree was still standing. It had survived another storm in its journey of life.

Dan and Pattie got out of the truck and walked around the Great Oak. Then out of the blue, a mist surrounded Dan and Pattie and then disappeared just as quickly as it appeared. Suddenly, Dan was on his knees proposing to Pattie. The ring was in the truck and after Pattie said yes, Dan retrieved the ring and placed it on her finger.

House hunting was put on the back burner. There were wedding plans to be made.

Dan announced his engagement to Pattie to his sons.

"Where are you going to live now Dad," Adam asked.

"I don't know," he answered honestly. "Pattie needs to be near work up north but I need to be near the lumber mill. And that's west. Then there's you and your fiancé."

"What about us?"

"Well, I'd like to be near any grandkids, hint, hint," Dan teased.

"We've got a few years yet. Don't rush me," Adam said. "Beside you should work on Jason and Taylor, they are ready to have kids."

"Well, that knucklehead better propose soon, or she's going to find someone else."

"Not to worry, Jason is waiting till after Peggy and I are married," Adam defended his brother. "He's just waiting for the right time. And right now, you and Pattie are the ones making the wedding plans."

CHAPTER SEVENTEEN

"...In hushed and happy twilight heard—
The treble of heaven's harmony—
These things he plants who plants a tree..."
--The Heart of the Tree, Henry Cuyler Bunner, 1912

"Dan, the invitations are ready to be sent out. Do you want to see it?" Lillian asked.

"No, mom, I am sure they are lovely. Just get them in the mail." Dan replied.

The invitation read:
Place: The First Presbyterian Church's Picnic Grove
Basking Ridge, New Jersey
Date: Saturday April 15, 2017
Time: 2PM to 5PM.
RSVP: Please respond by April 8, 2017

"I had a great response to the invitation. Only my sister Dana and her husband Ernie are unable to attend the reunion." Lillian informed Dan a week after sending the invitations.

"I think the reunion went very well and I loved all of the many family stories that were told. And Mom, it was great how you shared the story of the Basking Ridge postcard and how the family's DNA was part of the Great Oak Tree." Dan expressed with an emotional tone.

"Dan, you had everyone's attention when you pointed out the gravestones that held the Tilridge family name. Everyone seemed awed by the family history and how the Great Oak Tree impacted their family." Lillian replied.

"I loved the way hundreds of pictures were taken with the family members standing under the Great White Oak. They hugged the tree and each other." Dan said with a smile.

"Yes and everyone was sad to have the get together end. And a greater sadness was to know that next week, April 24, 2017, would begin the take down of the Great Oak Tree." Lillian responded.

As family members were leaving, sister Susan stopped and turned to Lillian and asked, "Did you or any of our other siblings ever find the book that Uncle Eli wrote about the family's history?"

Lillian said, "No and I wonder if Uncle Eli's book would hold the answers to Richard's and Sachi's family roots. I wonder where Mother stored it."

Janet, over hearing her sisters' conversation said, "I will gladly help you look for it, Lillian. Just let me know when and where we should start looking for it."

"Where, that is the big question?" Lillian asked herself.

2016

The Great Oak Tree Committee reread the findings to the public. It was the determination of a group of experts outside the community that the tree had died. In fact, had been dead for quite some time. For the safety of the people in the town, for the congregants and for the church structure, it had to come down. Since the tree was over 100 feet tall, about nine feet wide with a branch drip line of over 150 feet, taking it down would cost quite a bit of money, planning and man- and woman-hours of work.

The process was split into three parts. The planning or prep would take months. Pastor Tom as well as the mayor of Basking Ridge did their level best to assure the townspeople and anyone who was interested that no, there was no way to "save" the tree. And yes, the take down would be economically feasible, safe and transparent. The big event of taking down the tree, hauling it away along with cleanup, would be done in springtime. The exact date would be up to God who created it and the weather.

As if the Great White Oak knew its fate, she gave a glorious fall color display on her meager canopy.

STEP I - PREP

In a whirlwind of fundraising, Pastor Tom, members of the township, the historical society and the town representatives began the arduous task of collecting funds. There was of course the out and out begging. But after fundraisers, events, t-shirt and bake sales galore, enough money was collected to help offset the cost of the take down expenses. And that was if everything went well. Pastor Tom, a great observer of human nature knew that was pretty near impossible.

"It's going to be a PR nightmare," Dan said. "Not sure I really want to be a part of it."

"Aw, com'on," Ken said, waving a dismissive hand. "Sure, you do. This is the greatest job you'll ever be a party to."

"And if a branch falls on an innocent bystander or one of your crew?"

"Uh, that's where I come in," Gilly said. "I'm not saying that I've taken down a tree this huge but I have taken down trees in the Montreal suburbs where the streets are so narrow you can lean over and sip your neighbor's coffee. Through each other's windows."

"I don't know," Dan began.

"We can thread this needle," Gilly argued. "But we need your help. Your experience, your equipment--which only you know how to use and your common sense."

"There's no one else in this state, hell, even in this country that knows trees and lumber like you do."

"Don't flatter me," Dan said. "It's not going to change my mind."

"Don't make us talk to Pastor Tom," Gilly threatened.

"You wouldn't dare," Dan stiffened. He had a soft spot in his heart for the man who gently guided his wife Pattie through some tough times.

In the end, Ken and Gilly were persuasive and their arguments were sound. Dan was the third leg that held up the stool. Dan finally agreed. It almost took a year of planning which was filled with meetings, obtaining permits, arranging for additional equipment, addressing traffic flow and most important - safety issues.. In the logistics of taking down such a huge tree there had to be two cranes, and in talking about the weight, both cranes had to be set up to lift multi-ton weights of wood—not just any wood but solid white oak.

Ken and Gilly and Dan had teamed up with a crew of experienced loggers and lumbermen. The men, who spent more time in trees than on the ground, provided pages and pages of step-by-step tasks that had to be done in order to get the tree topped and sawn. With each cut there were at least three tasks that had to be done. Get the men high up into the tree, tie off and support the limb about to be cut, release any cables and plates previously attached that held the dying tree together. The ground crew would direct the men operating the cranes as well as the tree crew. They planned for each member of the cutting team to have two saws—their favorite reliable one and a backup saw. Everyone knew they'd be sawing into the unknown. The plans presented came along with some creative maneuvers to keep people away from the worksite. They also developed Plan B and Plan C to cover the what-ifs.

They would need the help of the entire town. For two days no one would really be able to go in and out of Basking Ridge the usual way. They had to block off Oak and Finley streets, traffic had to be rerouted. Dan needed to get in and out of the area without having to battle traffic, entering or exiting. And they had to have permits, which had to be submitted to the township.

State and local police had to be involved. Emergency medical teams needed to be put into place. The volunteer fire department. The Shade Tree Commission from Bernards Township was also notified. Although the oak technically was not a part of their shade tree project, as it had most certainly had been planted before 2012 when Hurricane Sandy knocked over 15,000 trees and prompted their development The Shade Tree Commission's goal was to replace and replant the many shade and street trees that Hurricane Sandy destroyed. Still, it was an acknowledgement of their love of trees and members were also invited to the front row. And wasn't it the township's largest shade tree that was being taken down?

There were also the specifications of the equipment. Dan's 40-ton boom truck was 9 feet wide and 34 feet long. The branches would have to be cut into pieces that would fit on the bed of his truck. The pieces would go to nearby facilities for milling and processing.

At the end of the meeting, Pastor Tom said, "Oh yes, don't forget about the steeple."

The foreman rubbed his eyes. "No problem, the crane operators will be made aware they can only swing in one direction, okay?"

"Thanks so much."

"Not like we're going to miss a 100-foot steeple," mumbled the foreman.

"It is 105 feet and 3 inches, to be exact," replied Pastor Tom.

The foreman nodded and gave the pastor a weak smile, as soon as Pastor Tom left the room, the foreman rolled his eyes. "Don't hit the steeple guys, the pastor will skewer us."

"Uh, yeah, it won't sit too well with God either."

2017

STEP II - TAKE DOWN

At four in the morning, it was cool, dark and misty and the perfect time for the first cup of coffee of the day. Dan looked out the window. Typical spring day in New Jersey. April 24 and the sun arrived right on time. Floodlights had been tossed up on the tree the night before and as soon as the crane trucks arrived, the take down process began.

The boom truck rumbled in the day of the take down. Dan knew he was literally going to be in town for four days, it was one thing to load and haul regular logs, but it was another to do it for a 600-year-old oak. He booked himself into the White House Inn near the center of town. His wife and mother would be staying with friends and family.

Temporary metal fencing was set up around the church. Church members were encouraged to show up and watch some of the process. They were given front row views behind the safety of the fence. Access was limited to allow for crowd movement. Dan had warned them. "Once I saw a scotch pine take down. The thing was taller than a skyscraper. No one anticipated the direction correctly enough to tell the farmer he needed to be over 100 yards away. Well, the cow got too close, and, well…"

There was a lottery of Guess the Weight, whose proceeds went into the general fund for the tree's takedown. There was only an informal first priority to church-goers to watch the take down and then regular citizens crowded behind them.

Pastor Tom explicitly warned everyone in his sermons on the Sunday prior, that no one would be permitted on church grounds. No one, not the mayor, not the press, not even the church secretary. Only those directly involved with the specific crews. Pastor Tom would be in the Church the whole time. Trimming branches took the most time. The tedious time-consuming, smaller branches, the width of a man's arm, had to be cut off. Dan forgot what it was like in his youth to clean up after a tree pruning something massive, the small branches were endless, they showered to the ground even with the slightest bump. Dan held his breath as a few escaped and bounced off the headstones below. The branches shattered on impact. Another indication of the tree being dead.

Progress was slow. Prior to each cut of a limb, the cables and any accompanying plates had to be disengaged and released. Some came apart easily and others were rusty and required copious amounts of WD-40.

CBS, USA Today, local New York and New Jersey reporters descended on the town. There were small press conferences in which the mayor, Pastor Tom and Ken read brief statements and answered a few questions.

Ken, Gilly and their teams' foremen as well as Pastor Tom were interviewed by local and national news organizations. Cameras were set up but not turned on. Not that they didn't want to stick around for the take down. But after finding out how grueling (and loud) the work would be, many simply did their interviews, left town and promised to return for the "big moment."

Congregants, of course, came early. Dan knew that many of them would be bored in about an hour. It was tedious work. It would look like to the general public, a lot of men and women standing around under the tree. At least you were able to be educated about how a tree is taken down and what a crane does, and what it doesn't do.

There were two cranes working on either side of the tree. Their tandem efforts had to be overseen by a foreman. The members of the ground crew were all wired for hands-free communication. All of them had to know where they should and shouldn't be. The crane operators were also aware of each other's movements. The larger crane was moving all the cut branches, some of them 30 feet long, onto the street for sawing. Dan positioned his boom truck on that side. Dan's first load was the large branch that faced east. The piece was lifted and laid in the street on top of planks for easier sawing and dismantling. They had to be sawn to the specific length and weight limits of Dan's boom truck. Dan moved the boom truck forward, loaded up and then moved the truck backward. The second branch was a smaller branch. Sawed into smaller, but more ragged pieces. He delicately loaded those as well. The third and fourth were larger branches. The biggest of the day was the seventh branch. A massive double branch with darkened crouch displaying signs of systemic decay. By branch number eight, Dan had to make his first haul away. This particular branch was huge. It was the branch that dipped down and touched the ground and curved back up toward the sky. The first cut was 60 feet above ground and the tree crew cut it into a "smaller" 25-inch diameter limb. The first step in the process.

If only people could just see this, they'd understand how necessary it was to take down this tree before it simply rotted and fell over. Or God forbid fell on someone's head. Even trees want to die with dignity, he thought.

It was nearly lunch time when Dan had to haul away his first load to the mill. The Great Oak was being chiseled away. By rough count, on day one 21 main branches were taken down. On the second day—the "easier" day - 13 main branches were taken down, in addition the massive tree trunk. That piece, Dan couldn't haul on his boom truck. They had planned to get the trunk on the flatbed of a tractor trailer. Piece by piece the tree shortened and shriveled. Reduced and diminished. But somehow it seemed to be a relief as though the person you loved had been hanging on for far too long.

That overwhelming feeling of guilt, comforted by the enormous impact they had on your life and the inability that you'd ever forget. You wanted to say: Let go. Your life was full and beautiful. Be at Peace.

After the truckloads were delivered to Dan's mill and another nearby mill, there was a lull. With each delivery and unloading, his spirit felt lighter—getting close to the end of a large project, but it also felt heavier. As much as he loved trees it was always hard to say good bye. Most especially to this grand old lady.

There were several issues. The saw team ruined three chainsaw chains when sawing at the main trunk. The tree crew cursed as he hit the cement almost 36 inches behind the bark. They thought they could peel away the wood which occluded around the enormous amounts of cement. But Ken and Gilly used the results of their sonograms to determine that it would be safer to saw as flush with the ground as possible. The cement was poured into the decaying cavity at a much higher level. Still, two more chains were destroyed as the saws hit a nail. The nail was a penny nail which probably tacked a broadside or poster to enlighten the citizens of Basking Ridge to news from the national or local government.

Around noon the teams had made their final felling cuts, they inserted the wedges and made the final test of the crane's cables. The crane heaved and there was a slight crack and a sigh as the tree's trunk was separated from its stump and roots.

The gathered crowd watched and applauded as the crane hoisted the massive trunk and laid it on the street in front of the Church. Over 25 tons, it lay like a great beast finally at rest.

STEP III- POST TAKE DOWN

Dan had been allowed to keep a piece of the wood, he wanted something from the Great Oak Tree to go directly to the church as a gift in memory of the Tilridge family. There seemed to be a lull in the work that needed to be done. The clean up after the felling of the tree took a day. Many people still wanted to come and get their picture taken standing on top of the tree stump. Some people scooped up handfuls of sawdust, others grabbed shards of oak. Some took twigs and others took old acorns that squirrels graciously left behind.

Dan wanted as many people as possible to receive a part of the Great Oak as memories of the tree. But Dan wanted more than sawdust, bookmarkers and pens. Then the Great Oak Tree Committee called Dan and asked if he wanted to have a commemorative CD of the process. The videography process was completed and before they "burn" a few hundred CDs," they wanted to know if Dan would be up for a private showing. It would be billed as Basking Ridge's Oscar Night. The private showing was also another fundraiser to help with the cost of the tree take down. Though not into the pageantry, Dan accepted the invitation. Pattie & Dan, Caroline (Pattie's Mother), Lillian & Brian, Adam & Peggy, Jason & Taylor, Katie and Lindsey dressed in formal attire for the event. The ladies wore their best gowns and the gentlemen wore tuxedos. The Committee even brought out a red carpet. Lots of pictures were taken. Local news crews of course were on hand. Apparently the take down of the massive oak tree was international news.

A following in Germany developed after die Gesund Baum, a German arborist company hired as the objective professionals, declared the tree dead; and that it was indeed a safety hazard. While they didn't like delivering the bad news, they were needed. The Great Oak Tree Committee knew they would have to go to outsiders in order to quell any conspiracy theories about possible conflict of interest. Especially among competing bidders in the Unites States and Canada for the job of a lifetime. Now it was not surprising, that more than a few European social media accounts followed any and all news of the Great Oak Tree.

Prior to the showing Dan, Ken and Gilly met with the web video editor. The Church also wanted to produce a time lapse "Documentary" of sorts of the tree project. It would be made available to the local schools as an education resource. Then they'd graciously post it on YouTube after a year of limited access for the entire world to see. Schools were also able to purchase an entire learning kit, complete with sawdust, an acorn and a DVD of the life and times of the 1619 Great White Oak Tree.

The pre-show meeting gathered all the men in the Church's conference room in the Willits House across the street from the church. Pastor Tom, while not a micro manager, was anxious that all the parties directly involved were not offended or put out by any of the footage or text. They hired a local voice actor to do the narration. The production was going

261

to be in the cameras that were recording in the church as well as cameras posted across the street.

"What the hell's that?" Dan made the tech guy stop the footage. One of the church's security cameras had been running after the massive tree was taken down. The marker showed 23:10 around eleven in the night. A blurriness gathered around the edges of the film and then coalesced within the cemetery. It seems to come from nowhere and yet appeared everywhere.

"Probably just a mist from the rain and humidity," said the IT guy. He shrugged. "Hey, this is New Jersey we're always used to mist." He turned back to look at the camera. Then he gulped.

The mist moved. It seeped in one direction and enveloped the stump. Gathering itself, it rose in a column. When it appeared to be about as high as one of the church windows, it stretched out its feathery fingers, and for a brief moment, became the shape of the oak tree. Then, it folded back into itself and then again with feathery fingers it crept along the ground and encircled each gravestone. Then dissipated. The IT guy let out a breath but then sucked it in. Rising from one of the headstones, a small, thin pillar of mist hovered. For many moments it wavered and pulsed. Dan estimated that it couldn't have been any taller than three feet. The small headstone it collected around was barely visible above the tree's remaining root. As the footage moved toward the 24:00 midnight marker, the tiny pillar condensed into a brighter almost shimmering cylinder shape. A wisp streamed up and came down. At 24:01 the mist simply disappeared.

The room was quiet. Then Dan said, "That was Martha Tilridge's gravestone, Mom was right about the Spirit of the Great Oak and its Soul." Finally, the secretary spoke up. "Do we edit that out?"

"No," Dan said. "Keep it in. We need to show folks every part of this."

"I don't know," Pastor Tom objected. "I don't want anyone to get freaked out by this misty phenomenon. I'd like to reflect on the positive aspects of the take down."

"You promised transparency," Dan reminded him.

"I did. But many people are anticipating the replanting of the 2001 baby white oak," Pastor Tom said. "You know the one grown from the acorns gathered in the cemetery years ago. I just don't want people to think it's all haunted here. I want them to visit and not be waiting for creepy mists."

"Fair enough," agreed Dan. "But we're not the only ones saying goodbye to the tree, are we?"

"No," Pastor Tom smiled. "I kind of hope we aren't."

In the back of the church, where tiny acorns thrummed and vibrated in the soil, there was another older song vibrating in the earth. Deep underground, a small tendril of fibrous root stretched out. Tiny hairs poked into the soil for nutrients and water. It grew. Sometimes when a thing has been growing for so long, it just doesn't understand the idea of death. It doesn't know that it is dead. It only knows how to grow. It does what it was made to do—grow.

Slowly over months and months, the roots of the mother tree reached out and touched the tiny acorn roots. Teasing them into germination, tiny roots intertwined and grew down splitting the shell in two while the seed leaves reached for sunlight above.

At the back of the church—just to the side—a not so massive tree is growing. It can be seen from the church's preschool parking lot. It's no different than any other white oak except that it is the daughter of the 619 year old Great Oak Tree. And deep in the ground, its roots tenderly curl around one of the ancient fibrous fingers, remaining connected eternally.

THE END

ACKNOWLEDGMENTS

It would be wrong of me not to thank some people that had a part in helping to write this book. First "Eeyore", without your guidance and willingness to get involved, the project would never have left the ground. So a big thank you! You know who you are. Second, my mom for helping with the little details to drive it over the finish line. Your patience and determination are unparalleled. Third, my wife and family for listening to me talk about the book over and over again. Finally, all my friends and customers for their continued support, kind words and encouragement along the way when I wanted to give up the pen.

All of you in total are "My Journey" and each of you make my life less ordinary! Thank you all!!!

P.S.: I still love my job.

The Storyteller's Note

The inspiration for this novel came from the discovery of a 1944 postcard of the historic Basking Ridge White Oak Tree in my grandparents' belongings. After researching the postcard, I recognized my enduring connection to this tree. Over generations, miles, catastrophes and wars this tree has sung its song to me. Though the tree is no longer standing, she lives on through people, folklore, musical instruments and keepsakes. She will be cherished for generations to come. I hope that the soul of this tree will sing on through these pages.

Listen to the wind in the trees my friends, they all have songs that need to be sung.

CPSIA information can be obtained
at www.ICGtesting.com
Printed in the USA
JSHW05042520922
30840JS00003B/15